POETS OF THE EARLY
SEVENTEENTH CENTURY

ROUTLEDGE ENGLISH TEXTS

GENERAL EDITOR: T. S. Dorsch, M.A.(Oxon.),
Westfield College, University of London

Volumes in the series include:

ELIZABETHAN LYRICAL POETS, edited by Patricia Thomson

ELIZABETHAN VERSE ROMANCES, edited by M. M. Reese

POETS OF THE EARLY SEVENTEENTH CENTURY, edited by
Bernard and Elizabeth Davis

DRYDEN: 'ABSALOM AND ACHITOPHEL' AND OTHER
SATIRES, edited by B. D. Greenslade

POPE: SATIRICAL POEMS, edited by J. Chalker

JOHNSON: 'RASSELAS' AND ESSAYS, edited by Charles Peake

WORDSWORTH: 'THE PRELUDE', BOOKS I-IV, edited by
P. M. Yarker

BYRON: 'DON JUAN', BOOKS I-IV, edited by T. S. Dorsch

POETS OF THE EARLY
SEVENTEENTH CENTURY

EDITED BY

BERNARD AND ELIZABETH DAVIS

ROUTLEDGE & KEGAN PAUL
LONDON AND BOSTON

First Published 1967
by Routledge & Kegan Paul Ltd.
Broadway House, 68-74 Carter Lane
London EC4V 5EL
and
9 Park Street
Boston. Mass. 02108
Reprinted 1972
By Unwin Brothers Ltd
Woking & London England

ISBN 0 7100 4511 5 (c)
ISBN 0 7100 4512 3 (p)

Contents

Introduction

This anthology is a representative selection of shorter poems written during the first half of the seventeenth century by principal poets of this period, Donne being excepted as his work is included in another volume of the series. Of these poets, only Ben Jonson in the strict sense was a professional author, writing as a means of livelihood. Milton and, probably, Browne, at this stage of their careers, were independent. The others pursued different professions, as courtiers, diplomats, tutors, clerics, and, in the case of Vaughan, as a physician. Most of these poems were probably fruits of their writers' leisure hours, and some at least were intended rather for private circulation than for early publication. With the notable exceptions of Milton's *Lycidas*, and *On the late Massacre in Piedmont*, two songs of Lovelace, and Marvell's *Horatian Ode*, none of the poems refers specifically to the political noises and conflicts of the period within which they were written. Pope's designation, in his Epistle *To Augustus*, 'the mob of gentlemen who wrote with ease', fits other poets of the age besides Suckling and the courtly lyricists, to whom he specifically applies it.

I THE HERITAGE IN POETRY

Seventeenth-century poetry, though affected inevitably by new forces and trends in a rapidly changing world, evolved without violent break from that of the age preceding it. Jonson's earliest plays and Donne's best-known poems were written before 1600; all Shakespeare's great tragedies were produced within the next few years. Milton confessed to Dryden that Spenser was his 'original', a statement fully confirmed by tributes to Spenser in Milton's prose works and echoes of Spenser, Browne, and other seventeenth-century Spenserians in his early poems. The partnership between music and lyrical poetry continued unbroken from the Elizabethan to the Jacobean era, with corresponding continuity in lyrical style and prosody, as can be seen in several of the poems which follow. Features most obviously differentiating seventeenth-century poetry from that of the Elizabethans, the school of Jonson from that of Spenser, suggest revaluation and adaptation rather than rebellion, both alike reflecting the many-sided culture, ancient and modern, Pagan and Christian, foreign and native, of the Renaissance. Throughout both periods, differences in mentality and usage notwithstanding, acceptance of ancient classical authors as masters in respect both of content and form served to inspire wholesale imitation of their works and, in the process, to maintain the cult of ideal patterns both in matter and in form. *The Faerie Queene*, the epic of Elizabethan humanism, follows a well-established Renaissance tradition, fashioning a gentleman, an ideal type of being, as hero of an epic, generally acclaimed as the ideal poetic genre. Seventeenth-century writers, no less than their precursors, are fascinated and confounded in contemplating 'what a piece of work is man'. But synthesis has given place to analysis, interest becoming centred less upon external attributes of the ideal type and more upon the inner being of man the microcosm, and the vagaries of individual personality. Under different aspects this tendency finds expression in Jonson's comedy of humours, prose characters like those of Earle's *Microcosmography*, psychological studies, notably Burton's *Anatomy of Melancholy*, and 'metaphysical poetry'.

2 PERSONALITY IN POETRY

All the poets here represented, in common with many contemporary prose writers, are self-expressive, and their poetry in this sense is personal, though in different ways and to different degrees. The autobiographical note recurs frequently throughout the work of Milton, from his earliest sonnet to *Samson Agonistes*. Herbert's *The Temple* consists, for the most part, of an extended 'confession', or self-examination in poetry. Herrick's personality is the life and soul of his work. Suckling and Lovelace, in light-hearted addresses to friends and mistresses, reveal themselves. The prominence of the personal note throughout the poetry of Jonson and of others following his lead certainly owes much to their reading and use of Latin poets, particularly Catullus, Horace, and Martial, but even allowing for this the general impulse for self-expression seems innate or intuitional, and not merely imitative. The enthusiasm of an earlier age was already spending itself before the turn of the century. Objectivity was giving place to introspection, new discoveries raised obstinate questionings; as Donne puts it:

> 'The new philosophy calls all in doubt,
> The element of fire is quite put out.'

Though none of the poems here under consideration is con-
cerned with either 'the new philosophy' foreshadowing the
genesis of modern science or the doubts arising from it, as a
whole they reflect diverse reactions to these uncertainties. In-
tellectual disquiet reveals itself in notes of scepticism, harping
on the familiar motive *carpe diem*, and, at an extreme, in
frank materialism and cynical mockery, as instanced in Suckling.
None the less, poets find abundant beauty and happiness in the
life of the world around them and genial intercourse with men
and women. The prevailing tone of their work is more gay than
grave.

3 SACRED POETRY

The very large output of religious poetry published during
this period may be attributed to several different influences;
more particularly to reaction against materialism, profanity, and
moral corruption in high places, the heat of religious controversy,
the study of theology and philosophy, and growing familiarity
with the Authorized Version of the Bible. No less remarkable
than the volume of religious poetry is the variety of forms in
which it is presented, and which include sacred epics, shorter
scriptural narrative poems, like Giles Fletcher's *Christ's Victory
and Triumph* (echoed in Milton's *Nativity Ode* and *Paradise
Regained*), didactic, argumentative, and reflective poems,
metrical versions of psalms, and hymns. The poetic level of such
work, as might be expected, is very uneven, ranging between
prosaic flatness and sudden bursts of lofty exaltation unsustained.
In this respect it is by no means exceptional, religious poetry of
all periods revealing all too clearly the difficulty of trying to
express the inexpressible, and the fact that sincerity of con-
viction, of itself, is not enough. Milton left unfinished his attempt
at a poem on the Passion, finding it 'to be above the years he had
when he wrote it, and nothing satisfied with what was begun'.

Many of Milton's contemporaries were less judicious, and
their work is forgotten. At its best, however, English religious
poetry of the seventeenth century reaches a higher level of
attainment than at any other period of its history. To attempt to
account for this fully is lost labour, for inspiration cannot be
measured or analysed; nevertheless the finest work of Herbert
owes much to the combined richness and purity of his language,

his resourcefulness in using imagery drawn from objects of everyday life, and his mastery of poetic form. The same may be said, with due adaptation, of Vaughan and Crashaw, each of whom draws imagery from the sources which most inspire him, Vaughan from cosmic nature, and Crashaw from the symbols of Catholic worship. Apart from poets whose work is predominantly sacred, the acceptance of a basic Christian faith, stated or implied, is widely revealed throughout the poetry of the period. The worldliness and frank sensuality of Herrick's *Hesperides* is offset by the 'natural piety' of *Noble Numbers*, and scriptural overtones are perceptible in Marvell's 'Mower' poems and *The Garden*.

4 NATURE IN POETRY

The use of external nature by seventeenth-century poets stems from the pastoral convention, well established in England, and greatly popularized by Sidney's *Arcadia* and the pastoral poems of Spenser. In this, as in other respects, the poetry of William Browne links the Elizabethans with their successors, and particularly with Milton, who in *Lycidas* borrows from both Browne and Spenser. Dr. Johnson remarked that Milton saw nature 'through the spectacles of books', which is certainly true of *Lycidas* and, up to a point, of *L'Allegro* and *Il Penseroso*. This comment could be applied pertinently to many other poets of this period.

It is not true, however, of Browne, whose pastorals, though compounded of traditional pastoral conventions, abound in natural description drawn first-hand from the scenery around his home in Devonshire. Here, as in other respects, Browne follows the lead of Spenser, who intersperses many descriptive passages throughout *The Faerie Queene*, but Browne's word-pictures are more extended and distinctively local and here he breaks new ground. In the course of the next half century the pastoral convention declined in popularity; but set against a new background and with characters decked in modern dress, it is still recognizable throughout Herrick's *Hesperides* and in Marvell's 'Mower' poems. On the other hand a considerable body of naturalistic poetry has little or no connection with pastoral, and Vaughan's treatment of nature as the witness of Divine immanence is the vision of an individual poet devoid of convention.

5 JONSON AND HIS SCHOOL

The two predominant influences perceptible throughout shorter poems of this period stem from the work of Jonson and Donne. In lyrical and non-dramatic poetry of all kinds, no less than in drama, Jonson was always a conscious artist and a highly successful one. His major achievement assessed from his poetry as a whole was to give new life to imitation by modifying and adapting it to native English tradition and usage. His epigrams, odes, songs, and other occasional poems are models of clarity, compactness, and symmetrical structure. He taught through example the intrinsic value of form in poetry. He supplied patterns followed directly or indirectly by numerous other poets with a wide diversity of talent, including Carew, Herbert, and Herrick, all of whom have inherited Jonson's sensitivity to this vital element in poetry, exploiting it in widely different ways with individual talent.

6 THE METAPHYSICAL POETS

The term 'metaphysical', applied to the poetry of Donne and his school, derives originally from a comment of Dryden that Donne 'affects the metaphysics'. Dr. Johnson, in his *Life of Cowley*, specifies at some length, with examples, salient characteristics of metaphysical poetry, violent combinations of dissimilar images, obscure allusions and comparisons, hyperbole, and far-fetched conceits, at the same time conceding that 'to write on their plan it was at least necessary to read and think'. The word *metaphysical*, which means 'concerned with the science of being', is strictly applicable only to a limited number of poets, for instance to Donne, Herbert, and Vaughan, but in practice it is commonly referred not merely to thought-content but to mannerisms of style, the latter, alike in Donne and his successors, showing extensive and ingenious exploitation of the art and resources of rhetoric. One does not have to read far in Herbert or Vaughan to realize that for the reader it is necessary to think. The seeming simplicity of Herbert's *Hope* or *The Pulley* conceals subtlety in underlying thought, rendered more complex through symbols; to appreciate and to understand the meaning of Vaughan's *Timber* or *The Waterfall* it is necessary to follow closely through his argument, taking into account overtones of meaning.

The thought-content of metaphysical poetry at its best is inseparable from the metaphysical style, but the degree of balance between them varies greatly as between different poems. Wit in understanding is matched by witty expression. Developed originally in reaction against the stale conventions of the Elizabethan pastoral poets and sonneteers, the metaphysical style at its worst degenerated to something far more artificial than the style which it superseded. The distinctive influences of Jonson and Donne, the neo-classical and the metaphysical, are mutually complementary. The discipline of the one counterbalances the freedom of the other, as this selection should show. Their final convergence appears most clearly in Marvell, chronologically the last of the group, whose poetry, while basically conforming with earlier traditions, prefigures at the same time the usage of a later age.

Brief critical comments on each poet and biographies will be found in the notes.

BEN JONSON

Inviting a Friend to Supper

To-night, grave sir, both my poor house and I
Do equally desire your company:
Not that we think us worthy such a guest,
But that your worth will dignify our feast
With those that come; whose grace may make that seem
Something, which else could hope for no esteem.
It is the fair acceptance, Sir, creates
The entertainment perfect, not the cates.
Yet you shall have, to rectify your palate,
An olive, capers, or some better salad   10
Ushering the mutton; with a short-leg'd hen,
If we can get her, full of eggs, and then,
Lemons, and wine for sauce; to these a coney
Is not to be despaired of, for our money;
And though fowl now be scarce, yet there are clerks,
The sky not falling, think we may have larks.
I'll tell you of more, and lie, so you will come:
Of partridge, pheasant, woodcock, of which some
May yet be there; and godwit if we can:
Knat, rail, and ruff too. Howsoe'er my man   20
Shall read a piece of Virgil, Tacitus,
Livy, or of some better book to us,
Of which we'll speak our minds, amidst our meat;
And I'll profess no verses to repeat:
To this, if aught appear, which I know not of,
That will the pastry, not my paper, show of.
Digestive cheese, and fruit there sure will be;
But that, which most doth take my Muse, and me
Is a pure cup of rich Canary wine,
Which is the Mermaid's now, but shall be mine: 30
Of which had Horace, or Anacreon tasted,
Their lives, as do their lines, till now had lasted.

Tobacco, nectar, or the Thespian spring,
Are all but Luther's beer, to this I sing.
Of this we will sup free, but moderately,
And we shall have no Pooly, or Parrot by;
Nor shall our cups make any guilty men:
But at our parting, we will be as when
We innocently met. No simple word,
That shall be uttered at our mirthful board,   40
Shall make us sad next morning: or affright
The liberty that we'll enjoy to-night.

From *Epigrams* (1616)

On My First Daughter

Here lies, to each her parents ruth,
Mary, the daughter of their youth;
Yet all heaven's gifts being heaven's due,
It makes the father less to rue.
At six months end she parted hence
With safety of her innocence;
Whose soul heaven's Queen, whose name she bears,
In comfort of her mother's tears,
Hath placed amongst her virgin-train,
Where, while that severed doth remain,   10
This grave partakes the fleshly birth,
Which cover lightly, gentle earth.

From *Epigrams* (1616)

On My First Son

Farewell, thou child of my right hand, and joy;
My sin was too much hope of thee, loved boy;
Seven years thou wert lent to me, and I thee pay,
Exacted by thy fate, on the just day.
O, could I lose all father, now! for why

Will man lament the state he should envy?
To have so soon scaped world's, and flesh's rage,
And, if no other misery, yet age!
Rest in soft peace, and ask'd, say here doth lie
Ben Jonson, his best piece of Poetry;   10
For whose sake henceforth all his vows be such,
As what he loves may never like too much.

From Epigrams (1616)

An Epitaph on S. P.: a Child of Queen Elizabeth's Chapel

Weep with me, all you that read
   This little story:
And know, for whom a tear you shed
   Death's self is sorry.
'Twas a child, that so did thrive
   In grace and feature,
As Heaven and Nature seemed to strive
   Which owned the creature.
Years he numbered scarce thirteen
   When Fates turned cruel,   10
Yet three filled Zodiacs had he been
   The stage's jewel;
And did act (what now we moan)
   Old men so duly,
As, sooth, the Parcæ thought him one,
   He played so truly.
So, by error, to his fate
   They all consented;
But viewing him since (alas, too late)
   They have repented;   20
And have sought (to give new birth)
   In baths to steep him;
But, being so much too good for earth,
   Heaven vows to keep him.

From Epigrams (1616)

To William Camden

Camden, most reverend head, to whom I owe
All that I am in arts, all that I know,
(How nothing's that?) to whom my country owes
The great renown and name wherewith she goes:
Than thee the age sees not that thing more grave,
More high, more holy, that she more would crave.
What name, what skill, what faith hast thou in things!
What sight in searching the most antique springs!
What weight, and what authority in thy speech!
Men scarce can make that doubt, but thou canst teach.　10
Pardon free truth, and let thy modesty,
Which conquers all, be once overcome by thee.
Many of thine this better could than I,
But for their powers, accept my piety.

From *Epigrams* (1616)

To John Donne

Donne, the delight of Phoebus and each Muse,
Who, to thy one, all other brains refuse:
Whose every work, of thy most early wit,
Came forth example, and remains so yet:
Longer a knowing than most wits do live,
And which no affection praise enough can give!
To it, thy language, letters, arts, best life,
Which might with half mankind maintain a strife;
All which I meant to praise, and yet I would;
But leave, because I cannot as I should.　10

From *Epigrams* (1616)

To Penshurst

Thou art not, Penshurst, built to envious show
Of touch, or marble, nor canst boast a row
Of polished pillars, or a roof of gold:
Thou hast no lantern, whereof tales are told,
Or stair, or courts, but stand'st an ancient pile,
And these grudged at, art reverenced the while.
Thou joy'st in better marks, of soil, of air,
Of wood, of water: therein thou art fair.
Thou hast thy walks for health, as well as sport:
Thy Mount, to which the Dryads do resort,   10
Where Pan, and Bacchus their high feasts have made,
Beneath the broad beech, and the chestnut shade;
That taller tree, which of a nut was set,
At his great birth, where all the Muses met.
There, in the writhed bark, are cut the names
Of many a Sylvane, taken with his flames,
And thence the ruddy Satyrs oft provoke
The lighter Fauns, to reach thy Lady's Oak.
Thy copse, too, named of Gamage, thou hast there,
That never fails to serve thee season'd deer   20
When thou would'st feast, or exercise thy friends.
The lower land, that to the river bends,
Thy sheep, thy bullocks, kine, and calves do feed:
The middle grounds thy mares and horses breed.
Each bank doth yield thee conies; and the tops
Fertile of wood, Ashore, and Sidney's copse,
To crown thy open table, doth provide
The purpled pheasant, with the speckled side:
The painted partridge lies in every field,
And, for thy mess, is willing to be killed.   30
And if the high-swoln Medway fail thy dish,
Thou hast thy ponds, that pay thee tribute fish,
Fat aged carps, that run into thy net,
And pikes, now weary their own kind to eat,
As loth the second draught or cast to stay,

Officiously at first themselves betray.
Bright eels, that emulate them, and leap on land,
Before the fisher, or into his hand.
Then hath thy orchard fruit, thy garden flowers,
Fresh as the air, and new as are the hours.   40
The early cherry, with the later plum,
Fig, grape, and quince, each in his time doth come:
The blushing apricot, and woolly peach
Hang on thy walls, that every child may reach.
And though thy walls be of the country stone,
They're reared with no man's ruin, no man's groan;
There's none that dwell about them wish them down;
But all come in, the farmer and the clown:
And no one empty-handed, to salute
Thy lord and lady, though they have no suit.   50
Some bring a capon, some a rural cake,
Some nuts, some apples; some, that think they make
The better cheeses, bring them; or else send
By their ripe daughters, whom they would commend
This way to husbands; and whose baskets bear
An emblem of themselves, in plum, or pear.
But what can this (more than express their love)
Add to thy free provisions, far above
The need of such? whose liberal board doth flow
With all that hospitality doth know!   60
Where comes no guest, but is allowed to eat,
Without his fear, and of thy Lord's own meat:
Where the same beer and bread, and self-same wine,
That is his Lordship's, shall be also mine.
And I not fain to sit (as some this day,
At great men's tables) and yet dine away.
Here no man tells my cups; nor, standing by,
A waiter, doth my gluttony envy:
But gives me what I call, and lets me eat,
He knows, below, he shall find plenty of meat;   70
Thy tables hoard not up for the next day,
Nor, when I take my lodging, need I pray

For fire, or lights, or livery: all is there;
As if thou, then, wert mine, or I reigned here:
There's nothing I can wish, for which I stay,
That found King James, when hunting late, this way,
With his brave son, the Prince, they saw thy fires
Shine bright on every hearth, as the desires
Of thy Penates had been set on flame
To entertain them, or the country came,   80
With all their zeal, to warm their welcome here.
What (great, I will not say, but) sudden cheer
Didst thou then make 'em! and what praise was heaped
On thy good lady then! who therein reaped
The just reward of her high huswifery;
To have her linen, plate, and all things nigh,
When she was far: and not a room, but drest
As if it had expected such a guest!
These, Penshurst, are thy praise, and yet not all.
Thy lady's noble, fruitful, chaste withal.   90
His children thy great lord may call his own:
A fortune, in this age, but rarely known.
They are, and have been taught religion; thence
Their gentler spirits have sucked innocence.
Each morn and even, they are taught to pray,
With the whole household, and may, every day,
Read, in their virtuous parents' noble parts,
The mysteries of manners, arms, and arts.
Now, Penshurst, they that will proportion thee
With other edifices, when they see   100
Those proud, ambitious heaps, and nothing else,
May say their lords have built, but thy lord dwells.

From *The Forest* (1616)

'Come, my Celia, let us prove'

Come, my Celia, let us prove,
While we may, the sports of love;
Time will not be ours for ever:
He, at length, our good will sever.
Spend not then his gifts in vain.
Suns that set may rise again;
But if once we lose this light,
'Tis, with us, perpetual night.
Why should we defer our joys?
Fame and rumour are but toys.   10
Cannot we delude the eyes
Of a few poor household spies?
Or his easier eyes beguile,
So removed by our wile?
'Tis no sin love's fruit to steal,
But the sweet theft to reveal:
To be taken, to be seen,
These have crimes accounted been.

        From *Volpone*, III. vii. 166–183 (1605)

'Kiss me, sweet: the wary lover'

Kiss me, sweet: the wary lover
Can your favours keep, and cover,
When the common courting jay
All your bounties will betray.
Kiss again: no creature comes.
Kiss, and score up wealthy sums
On my lips, thus hardly sundred,
While you breathe. First give a hundred,
Then a thousand, then another
Hundred, then unto the tother   10
Add a thousand, and so more:

Till you equal with the store,
All the grass that Rumney yields,
Or the sands in Chelsey fields,
Or the drops in silver Thames,
Or the stars that gild his streams,
In the silent summer-nights,
When youths ply their stol'n delights;
That the curious may not know
How to tell them as they flow,   20
And the envious, when they find
What their number is, be pined.

From *The Forest* (1616)

'Drink to me only with thine eyes'

Drink to me only with thine eyes,
    And I will pledge with mine;
Or leave a kiss but in the cup,
    And I'll not look for wine.
The thirst that from the soul doth rise
    Doth ask a drink divine:
But might I of Jove's nectar sup,
    I would not change for thine.
I sent thee late a rosie wreath,
    Not so much honouring thee,   10
As giving it a hope, that there
    It could not withered be.
But thou thereon did'st only breathe,
    And sent'st it back to me:
Since when it grows, and smells, I swear,
    Not of itself, but thee.

From *The Forest* (1616)

That Women are but Men's Shadows

Follow a shadow, it still flies you,
  Seem to fly it, it will pursue:
So court a mistress, she denies you;
  Let her alone, she will court you.
Say, are not women truly, then,
  Styled but the shadows of us men?

At morn and even shades are longest;
  At noon they are or short, or none:
So men at weakest, they are strongest,
  But grant us perfect, they're not known.   10
Say, are not women truly then
  Styled but the shadows of us men?

From *The Forest* (1616)

A Hymn to God the Father

Hear me, O God!
  A broken heart
  Is my best part:
Use still Thy rod,
  That I may prove
  Therein, Thy love.

If Thou hadst not
  Been stern to me,
  But left me free,
I had forgot   10
  Myself and Thee.

For sin's so sweet,
  As minds ill bent
  Rarely repent,

Until they meet
   Their punishment.

Who more can crave
   Than Thou hast done?
   That gav'st a Son
To free a slave,   20
   First made of nought,
   With all since bought.

Sin, death, and hell
   His glorious name
   Quite overcame;
Yet I rebel,
   And slight the same.

But I'll come in,
   Before my loss
   Me farther toss,   30
As sure to win
   Under His cross.
              From *Underwood* (1640)

A Celebration of Charis: Her Triumph

See the chariot at hand here of Love
   Wherein my Lady rideth!
Each that draws is a swan or a dove,
   And well the car Love guideth.
As she goes, all hearts do duty
   Unto her beauty;
And enamoured do wish, so they might
   But enjoy such a sight,
That they still were to run by her side,
Through swords, through seas, whither she would ride.   10

Do but look on her eyes, they do light
   All that Love's world compriseth!
Do but look on her hair, it is bright
   As Love's star when it riseth!
Do but mark, her forehead's smoother
   Than words that soothe her;
And from her arched brows, such a grace
   Sheds itself through the face,
As alone there triumphs to the life
All the gain, all the good of the elements' strife.   20

Have you seen but a bright lily grow,
   Before rude hands have touched it?
Have you marked but the fall o' the snow
   Before the soil hath smutched it?
Have you felt the wool o' the beaver?
   Or swan's down ever?
Or have smelt o' the bud o' the brier?
   Or the nard in the fire?
Or have tasted the bag of the bee?
O so white! O so soft! O so sweet is she!   30
            From *Underwood* (1640)

A Nymph's Passion

I love, and he loves me again,
   Yet dare I not tell who;
For if the nymphs should know my swain
   I fear they'd love him too;
   Yet if it be not known,
The pleasure is as good as none,
For that's a narrow joy is but our own.

I'll tell, that if they be not glad,
   They yet may envy me;

But then if I grow jealous mad,   10
   And of them pitied be,
   It were a plague 'bove scorn,
And yet it cannot be forborne,
Unless my heart would, as my thought, be torn.

He is, if they can find him, fair,
   And fresh and fragrant too,
As summer's sky, or purged air,
   And looks as lilies do
   That are this morning blown;
Yet, yet I doubt he is not known,   20
And fear much more, that more of him be shown.

But he hath eyes so round and bright,
   As make away my doubt,
Where Love may all his torches light,
   Though hate had put them out:
   But then, t'increase my fears,
What nymph soe'er his voice but hears
Will be my rival, though she hath but ears.

I'll tell no more, and yet I love,
   And he loves me; yet no   30
One unbecoming thought doth move
   From either heart, I know;
   But so exempt from blame
As it would be to each a fame,
If love or fear would let me tell his name.

                           From *Underwood* (1640)

On the Portrait of Shakespeare:
To the Reader

   This figure that thou here seest put,
   It was for gentle Shakespeare cut,

Wherein the graver had a strife
With nature, to out-do the life:
O, could he but have drawn his wit
As well in brass, as he hath hit
His face; the print would then surpass
All that was ever writ in brass:
But since he cannot, Reader, look
Not on his picture, but his book.   10

From the *First Folio Edition of*
Shakespeare's collected works (1623)

To the Memory of My Beloved, the Author, Mr. William Shakespeare: and what he hath left us

To draw no envy, Shakespeare, on thy name,
Am I thus ample to thy book and fame:
While I confess thy writings to be such,
As neither Man, nor Muse can praise too much.
'Tis true, and all men's suffrage. But these ways
Were not the paths I meant unto thy praise;
For seeliest ignorance on these may light,
Which, when it sounds at best, but echoes right;
Or blind affection, which doth ne'er advance
The truth, but gropes, and urgeth all by chance: 10
Or crafty malice might pretend this praise,
And think to ruin, where it seemed to raise.
These are, as some infamous bawd or whore
Should praise a matron. What could hurt her more?
But thou art proof against them, and, indeed,
Above the ill fortune of them, or the need.
I therefore will begin. Soul of the Age!
The applause! delight!—the wonder of our stage!
My Shakespeare, rise; I will not lodge thee by
Chaucer, or Spenser, or bid Beaumont lie   20

A little further, to make thee a room:
Thou art a monument without a tomb,
And art alive still, while thy book doth live,
And we have wits to read, and praise to give.
That I not mix thee so my brain excuses
I mean with great, but disproportioned Muses;
For if I thought my judgment were of years,
I should commit thee surely with thy peers,
And tell how far thou didst our Lyly outshine,
Or sporting Kyd, or Marlowe's mighty line;   30
And though thou hadst small Latin, and less Greek,
From thence to honour thee I would not seek
For names; but call forth thund'ring Aeschylus,
Euripides, and Sophocles to us,
Pacuvius, Accius, him of Cordova dead,
To life again, to hear thy buskin tread
And shake a stage: or when thy socks were on
Leave thee alone for the comparison
Of all that insolent Greece, or haughty Rome
Sent forth, or since did from their ashes come.   40
Triumph, my Britain, thou hast one to show,
To whom all Scenes of Europe homage owe.
He was not of an age, but for all time!
And all the Muses still were in their prime,
When, like Apollo, he came forth to warm
Our ears, or like a Mercury to charm!
Nature herself was proud of his designs,
And joyed to wear the dressing of his lines!
Which were so richly spun, and woven so fit,
As, since, she will vouchsafe no other wit.   50
The merry Greek, tart Aristophanes,
Neat Terence, witty Plautus, now not please;
But antiquated and deserted lie,
As they were not of Nature's family.
Yet must I not give Nature all: thy Art,
My gentle Shakespeare, must enjoy a part.
For though the poet's matter Nature be,

His Art doth give the fashion: and, that he,
Who casts to write a living line, must sweat,
(Such as thine are) and strike the second heat   60
Upon the Muse's anvil: turn the same,
(And himself with it) that he thinks to frame;
Or for the laurel he may gain a scorn,
For a good poet's made, as well as born.
And such wert thou. Look how the father's face
Lives in his issue, even so the race
Of Shakespeare's mind, and manners brightly shines
In his well turned, and true filed lines:
In each of which he seems to shake a lance
As brandisht at the eyes of ignorance.   70
Sweet Swan of Avon! what a sight it were
To see thee in our waters yet appear,
And make those flights upon the banks of Thames,
That so did take Eliza, and our James!
But stay, I see thee in the hemisphere
Advanced, and made a constellation there!
Shine forth, thou Star of Poets, and with rage,
Or influence, chide or cheer the drooping stage,
Which, since thy flight from hence, hath mourned like night,
And despairs day, but for thy volume's light.   80

From the *First Folio Edition of
Shakespeare's collected works* (1623)

To the Noble Lady, the Lady Mary Worth

I that have been a lover, and could show it,
    Though not in these, in rhymes not wholly dumb,
    Since I exscribe your sonnets, am become
A better lover, and much better poet.
Nor is my Muse or I ashamed to owe it
    To those true numerous graces, whereof some
    But charm the senses, others overcome

Both brains and hearts; and mine now best do know it:
For in your verse all Cupid's armory,
  His flames, his shafts, his quiver, and his bow,   10
  His very eyes are yours to overthrow,
But then his mother's sweets you so apply,
  Her joys, her smiles, her loves, as readers take
  For Venus' ceston every line you make.

From Underwood (1640)

From *A Pindaric Ode, to the Immortal Memory and Friendship of that Noble Pair, Sir Lucius Cary and Sir H. Morison*

    It is not growing like a tree
    In bulk, doth make man better be;
Or standing long an oak, three hundred year,
To fall a log at last, dry, bald, and sear:
        A lily of a day,
        Is fairer far, in May,
    Although it fall and die that night;
    It was the plant and flower of light.
In small proportions we just beauties see:
And in short measures life may perfect be.   10

From Underwood (1640)

'Queen and huntress'

Queen and huntress, chaste and fair,
  Now the sun is laid to sleep,
Seated in thy silver chair,
  State in wonted manner keep:
    Hesperus entreats thy light,
    Goddess, excellently bright.

Earth, let not thy envious shade
  Dare itself to interpose;
Cynthia's shining orb was made
  Heaven to clear, when day did close;   10
    Bless us then with wished sight,
    Goddess, excellently bright.

Lay thy bow of pearl apart,
  And thy crystal shining quiver;
Give unto the flying hart
  Space to breathe, how short soever:
    Thou that mak'st a day of night,
    Goddess, excellently bright.
        From *Cynthia's Revels*, V. vi. 1–18 (1600)

'Still to be neat'

Still to be neat, still to be dressed,
As you were going to a feast;
Still to be powdered, still perfumed:
Lady, it is to be presumed,
Though art's hid causes are not found,
All is not sweet, all is not sound.

Give me a look, give me a face,
That makes simplicity a grace:
Robes loosely flowing, hair as free:
Such sweet neglect more taketh me   10
Than all the adulteries of art;
They strike mine eyes, but not my heart.
        From *Epicoene, or The Silent*
        Woman, I. i. 122–133 (1609)

Ode (*to Himself*)

Come leave the loathed stage,
　　And the more loathsome age:
Where pride and impudence, in faction knit,
　　　Usurp the chair of wit!
Indicting and arraigning every day
　　　Something they call a play.
　　Let their fastidious, vain
　　Commission of the brain
Run on, and rage, sweat, censure, and condemn;
They were not made for thee, less thou for them.　　　10

Say that thou pour'st them wheat,
　　And they will acorns eat;
'Twere simple fury still thyself to waste
　　　On such as have no taste!
To offer them a surfeit of pure bread,
　　　Whose appetites are dead!
　　No, give them grains their fill,
　　Husks, draff to drink and swill.
If they love lees, and leave the lusty wine,
Envy them not, their palate's with the swine.　　　20

No doubt some mouldy tale,
　　Like Pericles, and stale
As the shrieve's crusts, and nasty as his fish—
　　　Scraps out of every dish
Thrown forth, and raked into the common tub,
　　　May keep up the Play-club:
　　There, sweepings do as well
　　As the best ordered meal.
For who the relish of these guests will fit
Needs set them but the alms-basket of wit.　　　30

And much good do't you then:
　　Brave plush and velvet-men

Can feed on orts; and, safe in your stage-clothes,
    Dare quit, upon your oaths,
The stagers and the stage-wrights too, your peers,
    Of larding your large ears
  With their foul comic socks,
  Wrought upon twenty blocks:
Which if they are torn, and turned, and patched enough,
The gamesters share your gilt, and you their stuff.   40

  Leave things so prostitute,
  And take the Alcaic lute;
Or thine own Horace, or Anacreon's lyre;
    Warm thee by Pindar's fire:
And though thy nerves be shrunk, and blood be cold,
    Ere years have made thee old,
  Strike that disdainful heat
  Throughout, to their defeat,
As curious fools, and envious of thy strain,
May, blushing, swear no palsy's in thy brain.   50

  And when they hear thee sing
  The glories of thy king,
His zeal to God, and his just awe o'er men:
    They may, blood-shaken, then
Feel such a flesh-quake to possess their powers
    As they shall cry, 'Like ours,
  In sound of peace or wars,
  No harp e'er hit the stars,
In tuning forth the acts of his sweet reign:
And raising Charles his chariot 'bove his Wain.'   60
               From *The New Inn* (1629)

WILLIAM BROWNE

'Glide soft, ye silver floods'

Glide soft, ye silver floods,
    And every spring:
Within the shady woods
    Let no bird sing!
Nor from the grove a turtle-dove
Be seen to couple with her love;
But silence on each dale and mountain dwell,
Whilst Willy bids his friend and joy farewell.

But (of great Thetis' train)
    Ye mermaids fair,
That on the shores do plain
    Your sea-green hair,
As ye in trammels knit your locks,
Weep ye, and so enforce the rocks
In heavy murmurs through the broad shores tell
How Willy bade his friend and joy farewell.

Cease, cease, ye murd'ring winds,
    To move a wave;
But if with troubled minds
    You seek his grave,
Know 'tis as various as yourselves,
Now in the deep, then on the shelves,
His coffin tossed by fish and surges fell,
Whilst Willy weeps and bids all joy farewell.

Had he Arion-like
    Been judged to drown,
He on his lute could strike
    So rare a soun',
A thousand dolphins would have come

And jointly strive to bring him home,   30
But he on shipboard died, by sickness fell,
Since when his Willy bade all joy farewell.

    Great Neptune, hear a swain!
      His coffin take,
    And with a golden chain
      For pity make
  It fast unto a rock near land!
Where every calmy morn I'll stand,
And ere one sheep out of my fold I tell,
Sad Willy's pipe shall bid his friend farewell.   40
From *Britannia's Pastorals*, Book II, Song I (1616)

'Venus, by Adonis' side'

Venus, by Adonis' side,
Crying kissed, and kissing cried,
Wrung her hands, and tore her hair
For Adonis dying there.

'Stay', quoth she, 'O stay and live!
Nature surely doth not give
To the earth her sweetest flowers
To be seen but for some hours.'

On his face, still as he bled,
For each drop a tear she shed,   10
Which she kissed or wip'd away,
Else had drown'd him where he lay.

'Fair Proserpina', quoth she,
'Shall not have thee yet from me;
Nor thy soul to fly begin
While my lips can keep it in.'

Here she closed again. And some
Say Apollo would have come
To have cured his wounded limb,
But that she had smothered him.   20
From *Britannia's Pastorals*, Book II, Song II (1616)

'*As careful merchants do expecting stand*'

As careful merchants do expecting stand,
After long time and merry gales of wind,
Upon the place where their brave ship must land:
So wait I for the vessel of my mind.

Upon a great adventure is it bound,
Whose safe return will valu'd be at more
Than all the wealthy prizes which have crown'd
The golden wishes of an age before.

Out of the East jewels of worth she brings;
Th' unvalued diamond of her sparkling eye   10
Wants in the treasures of all Europe's kings,
And were it mine they nor their crowns should buy.

The sapphires ringed on her panting breast
Run as rich veins of ore about the mould
And are in sickness with a pale possessed,
So true; for them I should disvalue gold.

The melting rubies on her cherry lip
Are of such power to hold, that as one day
Cupid flew thirsty by, he stooped to sip,
And fastened there could never get away.   20

The sweets of Candy are no sweets to me
When hers I taste; nor the perfumes of price,

Robbed from the happy shrubs of Araby,
As her sweet breath, so powerful to entice.

O hasten then! and if thou be not gone
Unto that wished traffic through the main,
My powerful sighs shall quickly drive thee on,
And then begin to draw thee back again.
From *Britannia's Pastorals*, Book II, Song III (1616)

Thyrsis' Praise of his Mistress

On a hill that graced the plain
Thyrsis sat, a comely swain,
    Comelier swain ne'er graced a hill:
Whilst his flock, that wandered nigh
Cropped the green grass busily,
    Thus he tuned his oaten quill:

'Ver hath made the pleasant field
Many several odours yield,
    Odours aromatical:
From fair Astra's cherry lip   10
Sweeter smells for ever skip,
    They in pleasing passen all.

'Leavy groves now mainly ring
With each sweet bird's sonneting,
    Notes that make the echoes long:
But when Astra tunes her voice,
All the mirthful birds rejoice,
    And are list'ning to her song.

'Fairly spreads the damask rose,
Whose rare mixture doth disclose   20
    Beauties pencils cannot feign;

Yet if Astra pass the bush,
Roses have been seen to blush,
   She doth all their beauties stain.

'Phœbus, shining bright in sky,
Gilds the floods, heats mountains high
   With his beams' all-quick'ning fire:
Astra's eyes, most sparkling ones,
Strikes a heat in hearts of stones,
   And enflames them with desire.   30

'Fields are blest with flow'ry wreath,
Air is blest when she doth breathe,
   Birds make happy every grove,
She, each bird, when she doth sing:
Phœbus heat to earth doth bring,
   She makes marble fall in love.'

                 From *England's Helicon* (1614)

'*A rose, as fair as ever saw the North*'

A rose, as fair as ever saw the North,
Grew in a little garden all alone;
A sweeter flower did Nature ne'er put forth,
Nor fairer garden yet was never known;
The maidens danced about it morn and noon,
And learned bards of it their ditties made:
The nimble fairies by the pale-faced moon
Water'd the root and kissed her pretty shade.
But well-a-day, the gard'ner careless grew;
The maids and fairies both were kept away,   10
And in a drought the caterpillars threw
Themselves upon the bud and every spray.
   God shield the stock! if heaven send no supplies,
   The fairest blossom of the garden dies.

               From *Visions*, published in
W. C. Hazlitt's edition of Browne's *Works* (1868–9)

Epitaph on the Countess Dowager of Pembroke

Underneath this sable hearse
Lies the subject of all verse:
Sidney's sister, Pembroke's mother:
Death, ere thou hast slain another,
Fair, and learn'd, and good as she,
Time shall throw a dart at thee.

Marble piles let no man raise
To her name: for after days
Some kind woman born as she,
Reading this, like Niobe   10
Shall turn marble, and become
Both her mourner and her tomb.

Included in Pembroke's *Poems* (1660)

Song of the Sirens

Steer hither, steer your winged pines,
    All beaten mariners.
Here lie Love's undiscovered mines,
    A prey to passengers;
Perfumes far sweeter than the best
Which make the Phoenix' urn and nest.
    Fear not your ships,
Nor any to oppose you save our lips;
    But come on shore,
Where no joy dies, till love hath gotten more.   10

For swelling waves our panting breasts,
    Where never storms arise,
Exchange; and be awhile our guests:
    For stars, gaze on our eyes.
The compass Love shall hourly sing,

And as he goes about the ring,
    We will not miss
To tell each point he nameth with a kiss.
    Then come on shore,
Where no joy dies till love hath gotten more.   20

From *The Inner Temple Masque* (1615)

ROBERT HERRICK

The Argument of his Book

I sing of brooks, of blossoms, birds, and bowers:
Of April, May, of June, and July-flowers.
I sing of may-poles, hock-carts, wassails, wakes,
Of bride-grooms, brides, and of their bridal-cakes.
I write of youth, of love, and have access
By these, to sing of cleanly-wantonness.
I sing of dews, of rains, and piece by piece
Of balm, of oil, of spice, and amber-grease.
I sing of times trans-shifting; and I write
How roses first came red, and lilies white.   10
I write of groves, of twilights, and I sing
The court of Mab, and of the Fairy-King.
I write of Hell; I sing (and ever shall)
Of Heaven, and hope to have it after all.

From *Hesperides* (1648)

Cherry-ripe

Cherry-ripe, ripe, ripe, I cry,
Full and fair ones; come and buy:
If so be, you ask me where
They do grow? I answer, There,
Where my Julia's lips do smile;
There's the land, or Cherry isle:
Whose plantations fully show
All the year, where cherries grow.

From *Hesperides* (1648)

Delight in Disorder

A sweet disorder in the dress
Kindles in clothes a wantonness:
A lawn about the shoulders thrown
Into a fine distraction:
An erring lace, which here and there
Enthrals the crimson stomacher:
A cuff neglectful, and thereby
Ribbands to flow confusedly:
A winning wave (deserving note)
In the tempestuous petticoat: 10
A careless shoe-string, in whose tie
I see a wild civility:
Do more bewitch me than when art
Is too precise in every part.

From *Hesperides* (1648)

Corinna's going a Maying

Get up, get up for shame, the blooming morn
Upon her wings presents the god unshorn.
  See how Aurora throws her fair
  Fresh-quilted colours through the air:
  Get up, sweet-slug-a-bed, and see
  The dew-bespangling herb and tree.
Each flower has wept, and bowed toward the east
Above an hour since; yet you not dressed,
  Nay! not so much as out of bed?
  When all the birds have Mattins said,   10
  And sung their thankful hymns: 'tis sin,
  Nay, profanation to keep in,
When as a thousand virgins on this day
Spring, sooner than the lark, to fetch in May.

Rise; and put on your foliage, and be seen
To come forth, like the Spring-time, fresh and green;
   And sweet as Flora. Take no care
   For jewels for your gown, or hair:
   Fear not; the leaves will strew
   Gems in abundance upon you: 20
Besides, the childhood of the day has kept,
Against you come, some orient pearls unwept:
   Come, and receive them while the light
   Hangs on the dew-locks of the night:
   And Titan on the eastern hill
   Retires himself, or else stands still
Till you come forth. Wash, dress, be brief in praying:
Few beads are best, when once we go a Maying.

Come, my Corinna, come; and coming, mark
How each field turns a street; each street a park   30
   Made green, and trimmed with trees: see how
   Devotion gives each house a bough,
   Or branch: each porch, each door, ere this
   An ark a tabernacle is
Made up of white-thorn neatly interwove;
As if here were those cooler shades of love.
   Can such delights be in the street,
   And open fields, and we not see't?
   Come, we'll abroad; and let's obey
   The proclamation made for May: 40
And sin no more, as we have done, by staying;
But, my Corinna, come, let's go a Maying.

There's not a budding boy, or girl, this day
But is got up, and gone to bring in May.
   A deal of youth, ere this, is come
   Back, and with white-thorn laden home.
   Some have despatch'd their cakes and cream,
   Before that we have left to dream:
And some have wept, and woo'd, and plighted troth,

And chose their priest, ere we can cast off sloth: 50
  Many a green-gown has been given;
  Many a kiss, both odd and even:
  Many a glance, too, has been sent
  From out the eye, love's firmament:
Many a jest told of the keys betraying
This night, and locks picked, yet we're not a Maying.

Come, let us go, while we are in our prime;
And take the harmless folly of the time.
  We shall grow old apace, and die
  Before we know our liberty.   60
  Our life is short; and our days run
  As fast away as does the sun:
And as a vapour, or a drop of rain,
Once lost, can ne'er be found again:
  So when or you or I are made
  A fable, song, or fleeting shade;
  All love, all liking, all delight
  Lies drown'd with us in endless night.
Then while time serves, and we are but decaying,
Come, my Corinna, come, let's go a Maying.   70

From *Hesperides* (1648)

The Captived Bee: or, the Little Filcher

As Julia once a slumb'ring lay,
It chanced a bee did fly that way,
(After a dew, or dew-like shower)
To tipple freely in a flower.
For some rich flower, he took the lip
Of Julia, and began to sip;
But when he felt he suck'd from thence
Honey, and in the quintessence:
He drank so much he scarce could stir;

So Julia took the pilferer.   10
And thus surprised, as filchers use,
He thus began himself to excuse:
'Sweet lady-flower, I never brought
Hither the least one thieving thought:
But taking those rare lips of yours
For some fresh, fragrant, luscious flowers,
I thought I might there take a taste,
Where so much syrup ran at waste.
Besides, know this, I never sting
The flower that gives me nourishing: 20
But with a kiss, or thanks, do pay
For honey that I bear away.'
This said, he laid his little scrip
Of honey 'fore her ladyship:
And told her, (as some tears did fall),
That, that he took, and that was all.
At which she smil'd; and bade him go
And take his bag; but thus much know,
When next he came a pilfering so,
He should from her full lips derive   30
Honey enough to fill his hive.

From *Hesperides* (1648)

To the Virgins, to make much of Time

Gather ye rose-buds while ye may,
Old Time is still a flying:
And this same flower that smiles to-day
To-morrow will be dying.

The glorious lamp of heaven, the sun,
The higher he's a getting:
The sooner will his race be run,
And nearer he's to setting.

That age is best, which is the first,
When youth and blood are warmer;   10
But being spent, the worse, and worst
Times still succeed the former.

Then be not coy, but use your time;
And while ye may, go marry;
For having lost but once your prime,
You may for ever tarry.

                              From *Hesperides* (1648)

His Poetry his Pillar

Only a little more
    I have to write,
    Then I'll give o'er,
And bid the world good-night.

'Tis but a flying minute,
    That I must stay,
    Or linger in it:
And then I must away.

O Time that cut'st down all!
    And scarce leav'st here   10
    Memorial
Of any men that were.

How many lie forgot
    In vaults beneath?
    And piece-meal rot
Without a fame in death.

Behold this living stone
    I rear for me,

Ne'er to be thrown
Down, envious Time, by thee.   20

Pillars let some set up,
   (If so they please)
   Here is my hope,
And my pyramides.

From *Hesperides* (1648)

The Hock-cart, or Harvest-home

Come, sons of summer, by whose toil
We are the lords of wine and oil:
By whose tough labours, and rough hands
We rip up first, then reap our lands.
Crowned with the ears of corn, now come,
And, to the pipe, sing harvest home.
Come forth, my Lord, and see the cart
Dressed up with all the country art.
See, here a maukin, there a sheet,
As spotless pure, as it is sweet: 10
The horses, mares, and frisking fillies,
(Clad, all, in linen, white as lilies.)
The harvest swains, and wenches bound
For joy, to see the hock-cart crown'd.
About the cart, hear, how the rout
Of rural younglings raise the shout;
Pressing before, some coming after,
Those with a shout, and these with laughter.
Some bless the cart; some kiss the sheaves;
Some prank them up with oaken leaves: 20
Some cross the fill-horse; some with great
Devotion stroke the home-borne wheat:
While other rustics, less attent
To prayers than to merriment,

Run after with their breeches rent.
Well, on, brave boys, to your Lord's hearth,
Glitt'ring with fire; where, for your mirth
Ye shall see first the large and chief
Foundation of your feast, fat beef:
With upper storeys, mutton, veal   30
And bacon, which makes full the meal,
With sev'ral dishes standing by,
As here a custard, there a pie,
And here all tempting frumentie.
And for to make the merry cheer,
If smirking wine be wanting here,
There's that, which drowns all care, stout beer;
Which freely drink to your Lord's health,
Then to the plough (the Commonwealth),
Next to your flails, your fanes, your fats;   40
Then to the maids with wheaten hats;
To the rough sickle, and crook'd scythe,
Drink, frolic boys, till all be blithe.
Feed, and grow fat; and as ye eat,
Be mindful, that the lab'ring neat,
As you, may have their fill of meat.
And know, besides, ye must revoke
The patient ox unto the yoke,
And all go back unto the plough
And harrow (though they're hang'd up now).   50
And, you must know, your Lord's word's true,
Feed him you must, whose food fills you:
And that this pleasure is like rain,
Not sent ye for to drown your pain,
But for to make it spring again.

From *Hesperides* (1648)

To Primroses filled with Morning-dew

Why do ye weep, sweet babes? can tears
    Speak grief in you,
    Who were but born
  Just as the modest morn
  Teem'd her refreshing dew?
Alas, you have not known that shower,
    That mars a flower;
    Nor felt the unkind
  Breath of a blasting wind;
  Nor are ye worn with years,   10
    Or warped, as we,
  Who think it strange to see
Such pretty flowers (like to orphans young),
To speak by tears, before ye have a tongue.

Speak, whimp'ring younglings, and make known
    The reason, why
    Ye droop, and weep;
  Is it for want of sleep?
  Or childish lullaby?
Or that ye have not seen as yet   20
    The violet?
    Or brought a kiss
  From that sweet-heart, to this?
  No, no, this sorrow shown
    By your tears shed
  Would have this lecture read,
That things of greatest, so of meanest worth,
Conceived with grief are, and with tears brought forth.

From *Hesperides* (1648)

To Anthea, who may command him anything

Bid me to live, and I will live
    Thy Protestant to be:
Or bid me love, and I will give
    A loving heart to thee.

A heart as soft, a heart as kind,
    A heart as sound and free,
As in the whole world thou canst find
    That heart I'll give to thee.

Bid that heart stay, and it will stay,
    To honour thy decree: 10
Or bid it languish quite away,
    And 't shall do so for thee.

Bid me to weep, and I will weep,
    While I have eyes to see:
And having none, yet I will keep
    A heart to weep for thee.

Bid me despair, and I'll despair,
    Under that cypress tree:
Or bid me die, and I will dare
    E'en Death, to die for thee.   20

Thou art my life, my love, my heart,
    The very eyes of me:
And hast command of every part,
    To live and die for thee.

From *Hesperides* (1648)

To Daffodils

Fair Daffodils, we weep to see
  You haste away so soon:
As yet the early-rising sun
  Has not attained his noon.
    Stay, stay,
  Until the hasting day
    Has run
  But to the Even-song;
And, having pray'd together, we
  Will go with you along.   10

We have short time to stay, as you,
  We have as short a spring;
As quick a growth to meet decay,
  As you, or any thing.
    We die,
  As your hours do, and dry
    Away,
  Like to the summer's rain;
Or as the pearls of morning's dew
  Ne'er to be found again.   20
           From *Hesperides* (1648)

The Mad Maid's Song

Good morrow to the day so fair;
  Good morning, sir, to you:
Good morrow to mine own torn hair
  Bedabbled with the dew.

Good morning to this primrose too;
  Good morrow to each maid,
That will with flowers the tomb bestrew,
  Wherein my Love is laid.

Ah, woe is me, woe, woe is me,
   Alack and welladay!   10
For pity, sir, find out that bee,
   Which bore my Love away.

I'll seek him in your bonnet brave:
   I'll seek him in your eyes;
Nay, now I think they've made his grave
   I'th' bed of strawberries.

I'll seek him there; I know, ere this,
   The cold, cold earth doth shake him;
But I will go, or send a kiss
   By you, sir, to awake him.   20

Pray hurt him not; though he be dead,
   He knows well who do love him,
And who with green-turfs rear his head,
   And who do rudely move him.

He's soft and tender (pray take heed),
   With bands of cowslips bind him;
And bring him home; but 'tis decreed,
   That I shall never find him.

                  From *Hesperides* (1648)

To Blossoms

Fair pledges of a fruitful tree,
   Why do ye fall so fast?
   Your date is not so past;
But you may stay yet here a while,
   To blush and gently smile;
     And go at last.

What, were ye born to be
  An hour or half's delight;
    And so to bid good-night?
'Twas pity Nature brought ye forth   10
  Merely to show your worth,
    And lose you quite.

But you are lovely leaves, where we
  May read how soon things have
    Their end, though ne'er so brave:
And after they have shown their pride,
  Like you a while: they glide
    Into the grave.

                    From *Hesperides* (1648)

His Content in the Country

Here, here I live with what my board
Can with the smallest cost afford.
Though ne'er so mean the viands be,
They well content my Prew and me.
Or pea, or bean, or wort, or beet,
Whatever comes, content makes sweet:
Here we rejoice, because no rent
We pay for our poor tenement:
Wherein we rest, and never fear
The landlord, or the usurer.   10
The quarter-day do's ne'er affright
Our peaceful slumbers in the night.
We eat our own, and batten more,
Because we feed on no man's score:
But pity those, whose flanks grow great,
Swelled with the lard of others' meat.
We bless our fortunes, when we see
Our own beloved privacy:

And like our living, where we're known
To very few, or else to none. 20
From *Hesperides* (1648)

The Night-piece, to Julia

Her eyes the glow-worm lend thee,
The shooting stars attend thee;
   And the elves also,
   Whose little eyes glow,
Like the sparks of fire, befriend thee.

No Will-o'th'-Wisp mis-light thee;
Nor snake, or slow-worm bite thee:
   But on, on thy way
   Not making a stay,
Since ghost there's none to affright thee. 10

Let not the dark thee cumber;
What though the Moon do's slumber?
   The stars of the night
   Will lend thee their light,
Like tapers clear without number.

Then Julia let me woo thee,
Thus, thus to come unto me:
   And when I shall meet
   Thy silv'ry feet
My soul I'll pour into thee. 20
From *Hesperides* (1648)

Upon Julia's Clothes

When as in silks my Julia goes,
Then, then (me thinks) how sweetly flows
That liquefaction of her clothes.

Next, when I cast mine eyes and see
That brave vibration each way free;
O how that glittering taketh me!

From *Hesperides* (1648)

An Ode for Ben Jonson

Ah Ben!
Say how, or when
Shall we thy guests
Meet at those lyric feasts,
Made at the Sun,
The Dog, the triple Tun?
Where we such clusters had,
As made us nobly wild, not mad;
And yet each verse of thine
Out-did the meat, out-did the frolic wine.   10

My Ben
Or come agen:
Or send to us
Thy wit's great over-plus;
But teach us yet
Wisely to husband it;
Lest we that talent spend:
And having once brought to an end
That precious stock, the store
Of such a wit the world should have no more.   20

From *Hesperides* (1648)

His Litany, to the Holy Spirit

In the hour of my distress,
When temptations me oppress,
And when I my sins confess,
    Sweet Spirit, comfort me!

When I lie within my bed,
Sick in heart, and sick in head,
And with doubts discomforted,
    Sweet Spirit, comfort me!

When the house doth sigh and weep,
And the world is drown'd in sleep,   10
Yet mine eyes the watch do keep;
    Sweet Spirit, comfort me!

When the artless doctor sees
No one hope, but of his fees,
And his skill runs on the lees:
    Sweet Spirit, comfort me!

When his potion and his pill,
His, or none, or little skill,
Meet for nothing, but to kill;
    Sweet Spirit, comfort me!   20

When the passing-bell doth toll,
And the furies in a shoal
Come to fright a parting soul:
    Sweet Spirit, comfort me!

When the tapers now burn blue,
And the comforters are few,
And that number more than true:
    Sweet Spirit, comfort me!

When the priest his last hath pray'd,
And I nod to what is said,   30
'Cause my speech is now decay'd
 Sweet Spirit, comfort me!

When, God knows, I'm tossed about,
Either with despair, or doubt;
Yet before the glass be out,
 Sweet Spirit, comfort me!

When the Tempter me pursu'th
With the sins of all my youth,
And half damns me with untruth:
 Sweet Spirit, comfort me!   40

When the flames and hellish cries
Fright mine ears, and fright mine eyes,
And all terrors me surprise;
 Sweet Spirit, comfort me!

When the Judgment is revealed,
And that open'd which was sealed,
When to Thee I have appealed,
 Sweet Spirit, comfort me!

From Noble Numbers (1648)

A Thanksgiving to God, for his House

Lord, Thou hast given me a cell
 Wherein to dwell;
And little house, whose humble roof
 Is weather-proof;
Under the spars of which I lie
 Both soft, and dry;

Where Thou my chamber for to ward
    Hast set a guard
Of harmless thoughts, to watch and keep
    Me, while I sleep.   10
Low is my porch, as is my fate,
    Both void of state;
And yet the threshold of my door
    Is worn by the poor,
Who thither come, and freely get
    Good words, or meat:
Like as my parlour, so my hall
    And kitchen's small:
A little buttery, and therein
    A little bin,   20
Which keeps my little loaf of bread
    Unchipped, unflead:
Some brittle sticks of thorn or briar
    Make me a fire,
Close by whose living coal I sit,
    And glow like it.
Lord, I confess too, when I dine,
    The pulse is Thine,
And all those other bits that be
    There placed by Thee;   30
The worts, the purslane, and the mess
    Of water-cress,
Which of Thy kindness Thou hast sent;
    And my content
Make those, and my beloved beet
    To be more sweet.
'Tis Thou that crown'st my glittering hearth
    With guiltless mirth;
And giv'st me wassail bowls to drink,
    Spic'd to the brink.   40
Lord, 'tis Thy plenty-dropping hand
    That soils my land;

And giv'st me, for my bushel sown,
 Twice ten for one:
That mak'st my teeming hen to lay
 Her egg each day:
Besides my healthful ewes to bear
 Me twins each year:
The while the conduits of my kine
 Run cream (for wine).   50
All these, and better Thou dost send
 Me, to this end,
That I should render, for my part,
 A thankful heart;
Which, fired with incense, I resign,
 As wholly Thine;
But the acceptance, that must be,
 My Christ, by Thee.

      From *Noble Numbers* (1648)

Grace for a Child

Here a little child I stand,
Heaving up my either hand:
Cold as paddocks though they be,
Here I lift them up to Thee,
For a benison to fall
On our meat, and on us all. Amen.

      From *Noble Numbers* (1648)

GEORGE HERBERT

The Church Floor

Mark you the floor? that square and speckled stone,
     Which looks so firm and strong,
         Is Patience;

And the other black and grave, wherewith each one
     Is checkered all along,
         Humility.

The gentle rising, which on either hand
     Leads to the quire above,
         Is Confidence;

But the sweet cement, which in one sure band   10
     Ties the whole frame, is Love
         And Charity.

Hither sometimes Sin steals, and stains
  The marble's neat and curious veins;
But all is cleansed when the marble weeps.
  Sometimes Death, puffing at the door,
  Blows all the dust about the floor;
But while he thinks to spoil the room, he sweeps.
  Blest be the Architect, whose art
  Could build so strong in a weak heart.   20
             From *The Temple* (1633)

The Windows

Lord, how can man preach Thy eternal Word?
     He is a brittle crazy glass:

Yet in Thy temple Thou dost him afford
    This glorious and transcendent place,
    To be a window, through Thy grace.

But when Thou dost anneal in glass Thy story,
    Making Thy life to shine within
The holy preachers; then the light and glory
    More reverend grows, and more doth win;
    Which else shows waterish, bleak, and thin.   10

Doctrine and life, colours and light, in one
    When they combine and mingle, bring
A strong regard and awe; but speech alone
    Doth vanish like a flaring thing,
    And in the ear, not conscience, ring.

                    From *The Temple* (1633)

The Altar

A broken ALTAR, Lord, Thy servant rears,
Made of a heart, and cemented with tears;
    Whose parts are as Thy hand did frame;
    No workman's tool hath touch'd the same.
          A   HEART   alone
          Is   such   a   stone,
          As   nothing   but
          Thy   power   doth   cut.
          Wherefore   each   part
          Of   my   hard   heart   10
          Meets   in   this   frame,
          To   praise   Thy   name:
    That, if I chance to hold my peace,
    These stones to praise Thee may not cease.
O let Thy blessed SACRIFICE be mine,
And sanctify this ALTAR to be Thine.

                    From *The Temple* (1633)

Easter

Rise, heart; thy Lord is risen. Sing His praise
        Without delays,
Who takes thee by the hand, that thou likewise
        With Him may'st rise;
That, as His death calcined thee to dust,
His life may make thee gold, and much more, just.

Awake, my lute, and struggle for my part
        With all thy art.
The cross taught all wood to resound His name,
        Who bore the same.   10
His stretched sinews taught all strings what key
Is best to celebrate this most high day.

Consort both heart and lute, and twist a song
        Pleasant and long;
Or since all music is but three parts vied,
        And multiplied,
O let Thy blessed Spirit bear a part,
And make up our defects with His sweet art.

    I got me flowers to strew Thy way;
    I got me boughs off many a tree;   20
    But Thou wast up by break of day,
    And brought'st Thy sweets along with Thee.

    The sun arising in the east,
    Though he give light, and th'east perfume;
    If they should offer to contest
    With Thy arising, they presume.

    Can there be any day but this,
    Though many suns to shine endeavour?
    We count three hundred, but we miss:
    There is but one, and that one ever.   30
            From *The Temple* (1633)

Easter Wings

Lord, who createdst man in wealth and store,
  Though foolishly he lost the same,
    Decaying more and more,
      Till he became
      Most poor;
      With Thee
      O let me rise
    As larks, harmoniously,
  And sing this day Thy victories:
Then shall the fall further the flight in me.   10

My tender age in sorrow did begin:
  And still with sicknesses and shame
    Thou did'st so punish sin,
      That I became
      Most thin.
      With Thee
      Let me combine
    And feel this day Thy victory;
  For, if I imp my wing on Thine,
Affliction shall advance the flight in me.   20
              From *The Temple* (1633)

Redemption

Having been tenant long to a rich Lord,
  Not thriving, I resolved to be bold,
  And make a suit unto Him, to afford
A new small-rented lease, and cancel the old.
In Heaven at His manor I Him sought:
  They told me there, that He was lately gone
  About some land, which He had dearly bought
Long since on earth, to take possession.

I straight returned, and knowing His great birth,
   Sought Him accordingly in great resorts;   10
   In cities, theatres, gardens, parks and courts:
At length I heard a ragged noise and mirth
   Of thieves and murderers; there I Him espied,
   Who straight, 'Your suit is granted,' said, and died.
                  From *The Temple* (1633)

Jordan

Who says that fictions only and false hair
Become a verse? Is there in truth no beauty?
Is all good structure in a winding stair?
May no lines pass, except they do their duty
   Not to a true, but painted chair?

Is it no verse, except enchanted groves
And sudden arbours shadow coarse-spun lines?
Must purling streams refresh a lover's loves?
Must all be veiled, while he that reads, divines,
   Catching the sense at two removes?   10

Shepherds are honest people; let them sing:
Riddle who list, for me, and pull for prime:
I envy no man's nightingale or spring;
Nor let them punish me with loss of rhyme,
   Who plainly say, 'My God, my King!'
                  From *The Temple* (1633)

Avarice

Money, thou bane of bliss and source of woe,
   Whence com'st thou, that thou art so fresh and fine?
   I know thy parentage is base and low:
Man found thee poor and dirty in a mine.

Surely thou didst so little contribute
  To this great kingdom, which thou now hast got,
  That he was fain, when thou wert destitute,
To dig thee out of thy dark cave and grot.
Then forcing thee, by fire he made thee bright:
  Nay, thou hast got the face of man; for we   10
  Have with our stamp and seal transferred our right:
Thou art the man, and man but dross to thee.
  Man calleth thee his wealth, who made thee rich;
  And while he digs out thee, falls in the ditch.

From The Temple (1633)

The World

Love built a stately house, where Fortune came,
And spinning fancies, she was heard to say
That her fine cobwebs did support the frame,
Whereas they were supported by the same;
But Wisdom quickly swept them all away.

Then Pleasure came, who, liking not the fashion,
Began to make balconies, terraces,
Till she had weakened all by alteration;
But reverend laws, and many a proclamation
Reformed all at length with menaces.   10

Then entered Sin, and with that sycamore,
Whose leaves first sheltered man from drought and dew,
Working and winding slily evermore,
The inward walls and summers cleft and tore;
But Grace shored these, and cut that as it grew.

Then Sin combined with Death in a firm band
To raze the building to the very floor:
Which they effected, none could them withstand.
But Love and Grace took Glory by the hand,
And built a braver palace than before.   20

From The Temple (1633)

Virtue

Sweet day, so cool, so calm, so bright,
The bridal of the earth and sky,
The dew shall weep thy fall to night;
    For thou must die.

Sweet rose, whose hue, angry and brave,
Bids the rash gazer wipe his eye,
Thy root is ever in its grave,
    And thou must die.

Sweet Spring, full of sweet days and roses,
A box where sweets compacted lie,   10
My music shows ye have your closes,
    And all must die.

Only a sweet and virtuous soul,
Like season'd timber, never gives;
But though the whole world turn to coal,
    Then chiefly lives.

               From *The Temple* (1633)

Unkindness

Lord, make me coy and tender to offend:
In friendship first, I think, if that agree,
      Which I intend,
   Unto my friend's intent and end.
I would not use a friend as I use Thee.

If any touch my friend or his good name,
It is my honour and my love to free
      His blasted fame
   From the least spot or thought of blame.
I could not use a friend as I use Thee.   10

My friend may spit upon my curious floor:
Would he have gold? I lend it instantly;
    But let the poor,
  And Thou within them, starve at door.
I cannot use a friend as I use Thee.

When that my friend pretendeth to a place,
I quit my interest, and leave it free;
    But when Thy grace
  Sues for my heart, I Thee displace;
Nor would I use a friend as I use Thee.   20

Yet can a friend what Thou hast done fulfil?
O write in brass: 'My God upon a tree
    His blood did spill,
  Only to purchase my good will.'
Yet use I not my foes as I use Thee.
From The Temple (1633)

Life

I made a posy, while the day ran by:
Here will I smell my remnant out, and tie
    My life with this band.
But Time did beckon to the flowers, and they
By noon most cunningly did steal away,
    And wither'd in my hand.

My hand was next to them, and then my heart:
I took, without more thinking, in good part
    Time's gentle admonition;
Who did so sweetly death's sad taste convey,   10
Making my mind to smell my fatal day;
    Yet sugaring the suspicion.

Farewell, dear flowers, sweetly your time ye spent,
Fit, while ye lived, for smell or ornament,
    And after death for cures.
I follow straight without complaints or grief,
Since, if my scent be good, I care not if
    It be as short as yours.

                From *The Temple* (1633)

The Quip

The merry world did on a day
With his train-bands and mates agree
To meet together, where I lay,
And all in sport to jeer at me.

First, Beauty crept into a rose;
Which when I plucked not, 'Sir,' said she,
'Tell me, I pray, whose hands are those?'
But Thou shalt answer, Lord, for me.

Then Money came, and chinking still,
'What tune is this, poor man?' said he: 10
'I heard in music you had skill.'
But Thou shalt answer, Lord, for me.

Then came brave Glory puffing by
In silks that whistled, who but he?
He scarce allow'd me half an eye.
But Thou shalt answer, Lord, for me.

Then came quick Wit and Conversation,
And he would needs a comfort be,
And, to be short, made an Oration.
But Thou shalt answer, Lord, for me.   20

Yet when the hour of Thy design
To answer these fine things shall come,
Speak not at large; say 'I am thine.'
And then they have their answer home.

From *The Temple* (1633)

Hope

I gave to Hope a watch of mine; but he
      An anchor gave to me.
Then an old prayer-book I did present;
      And he an optic sent.
With that I gave a vial full of tears;
      But he a few green ears.
Ah, loiterer! I'll no more, no more I'll bring:
      I did expect a ring.

From *The Temple* (1633)

Time

Meeting with Time, 'Slack thing,' said I,
'Thy scythe is dull; whet it, for shame.'
'No marvel, sir,' he did reply,
'If it at length deserve some blame;
   But where one man would have me grind it,
   Twenty for one too sharp do find it.'

'Perhaps some such of old did pass,
Who above all things lov'd this life;
To whom thy scythe a hatchet was,
Which now is but a pruning knife.   10
   Christ's coming hath made man thy debtor,
   Since by thy cutting he grows better.

'And in His blessing thou art blest;
For where thou only wert before
An executioner at best,
Thou art a gardener now, and more,
   An usher to convey our souls
   Beyond the utmost stars and poles.

'And this is that makes life so long,
While it detains us from our God.   20
E'en pleasures here increase the wrong,
And length of days lengthen the rod.
   Who wants the place, where God doth dwell,
   Partakes already half of hell.

'Of what strange length must that needs be,
Which e'en eternity excludes!'
Thus far Time heard me patiently;
Then chafing said, 'This man deludes:
   What do I here before his door?
   He doth not crave less time, but more.'   30

From *The Temple* (1633)

Peace

Sweet Peace, where dost thou dwell? I humbly crave,
    Let me once know.
  I sought thee in a secret cave,
    And asked if Peace were there.
A hollow wind did seem to answer, 'No:
    Go seek elsewhere.'

I did; and going did a rainbow note.
    'Surely,' thought I,
  'This is the lace of Peace's coat;
    I will search out the matter.'   10

But while I looked, the clouds immediately
     Did break and scatter.

Then went I to a garden, and did spy
     A gallant flower,
  The crown imperial. 'Sure,' said I,
     'Peace at the root must dwell.'
But when I digg'd, I saw a worm devour
     What show'd so well.

At length I met a reverend good old man,
     Whom when for Peace   20
  I did demand, he thus began:
     'There was a Prince of old
At Salem dwelt, who liv'd with good increase
     Of flock and fold.

'He sweetly lived; yet sweetness did not save
     His life from foes.
  But after death out of His grave
     There sprang twelve stalks of wheat;
Which many wondering at, got some of those
     To plant and set.   30

'It prospered strangely, and did soon disperse
     Through all the earth;
  For they that taste it do rehearse
     That virtue lies therein;
A secret virtue, bringing peace and mirth
     By flight of sin.

'Take of this grain, which in my garden grows,
     And grows for you;
  Make bread of it; and that repose
     And peace, which everywhere   40
With so much earnestness you do pursue,
     Is only there.'

From *The Temple* (1633)

The Storm

If as the winds and waters here below
            Do fly and flow,
My sighs and tears as busy were above,
            Sure they would move
And much affect Thee, as tempestuous times
Amaze poor mortals, and object their crimes.

Stars have their storms, ev'n in a high degree,
            As well as we.
A throbbing conscience spurred by remorse
            Hath a strange force: 10
It quits the earth, and mounting more and more,
Dares to assault Thee, and besiege Thy door.

There it stands knocking, to thy music's wrong,
            And drowns the song.
Glory and honour are set by, till it
            An answer get.
Poets have wronged poor storms: such days are best;
They purge the air without; within, the breast.

                          From *The Temple* (1633)

The Pilgrimage

I travelled on, seeing the hill where lay
            My expectation.
      A long it was and weary way.
      The gloomy cave of Desperation
I left on the one, and on the other side
            The rock of Pride.

And so I came to Fancy's meadow, strow'd
            With many a flower:

Fain would I here have made abode,
But I was quickened by my hour.   10
So to Care's copse I came, and there got through
     With much ado.

That led me to the wild of Passion, which
     Some call the wold;
A wasted place, but sometimes rich.
Here I was robbed of all my gold,
Save one good angel, which a friend had tied
     Close to my side.

At length I got unto the gladsome hill,
     Where lay my hope,   20
     Where lay my heart; and climbing still,
When I had gained the brow and top,
A lake of brackish waters on the ground
     Was all I found.

With that, abash'd and struck with many a sting
     Of swarming fears,
     I fell, and cried, 'Alas, my King!
Can both the way and end be tears?'
Yet taking heart I rose, and then perceiv'd
     I was deceiv'd.   30

My hill was further; so I flung away,
     Yet heard a cry
     Just as I went, 'None goes that way
And lives.' 'If that be all,' said I,
'After so foul a journey death is fair,
     And but a chair.'

From *The Temple* (1633)

The Collar

I struck the board and cried, 'No more!
        I will abroad.
   What? shall I ever sigh and pine?
My lines and life are free; free as the road,
    Loose as the wind, as large as store.
       Shall I be still in suit?
    Have I no harvest but a thorn
    To let me blood, and not restore
What I have lost with cordial fruit?
       Sure there was wine   10
Before my sighs did dry it: there was corn
     Before my tears did drown it.
    Is the year only lost to me?
     Have I no bays to crown it?
No flowers, no garlands gay? All blasted?
      All wasted?
   Not so, my heart; but there is fruit,
     And thou hast hands.
    Recover all thy sigh-blown age
On double pleasures: leave thy cold dispute   20
Of what is fit, and not; forsake thy cage,
     Thy rope of sands,
Which petty thoughts have made, and made to thee
   Good cable, to enforce and draw,
     And be thy law,
While thou didst wink and wouldst not see.
     Away, take heed:
     I will abroad.
Call in thy death's head there: tie up thy fears.
     He that forbears   30
    To suit and serve his need,
     Deserves his load.'
But as I raved and grew more fierce and wild
     At every word,

Methought I heard one calling, 'Child!'
And I replied, 'My Lord!'

From *The Temple* (1633)

The Pulley

When God at first made man,
Having a glass of blessings standing by,
'Let us,' said He, 'pour on him all we can:
Let the world's riches, which dispersed lie,
        Contract into a span.'

So Strength first made a way;
Then Beauty flowed, then Wisdom, Honour, Pleasure:
When almost all was out, God made a stay,
Perceiving that alone of all His treasure
        Rest in the bottom lay.   10

'For if I should,' said He,
'Bestow this jewel also on My creature,
He would adore My gifts instead of Me,
And rest in Nature, not the God of Nature:
        So both should losers be.

'Yet let him keep the rest,
But keep them with repining restlessness:
Let him be rich and weary, that at least,
If goodness lead him not, yet weariness
        May toss him to My breast.'   20

From *The Temple* (1633)

Aaron

Holiness on the head,
Light and perfections on the breast,
Harmonious bells below, raising the dead
To lead them unto life and rest:
Thus are true Aarons drest.

Profaneness in my head,
Defects and darkness in my breast,
A noise of passions ringing me for dead
Unto a place where is no rest:
Poor priest, thus am I drest.   10

Only another head,
I have, another heart and breast,
Another music, making live not dead,
Without whom I could have no rest:
In Him I am well drest.

Christ is my only head,
My alone only heart and breast,
My only music, striking me ev'n dead:
That to the old man I may rest,
And be in Him new drest.   20

So holy in my head,
Perfect and light in my dear breast,
My doctrine tun'd by Christ, (who is not dead,
But lives in me while I do rest),
Come, people; Aaron's drest.

From *The Temple* (1633)

Discipline

Throw away Thy rod,
Throw away Thy wrath:
   O my God,
Take the gentle path.

For my heart's desire
Unto Thine is bent:
   I aspire
To a full consent.

Not a word or look
I affect to own,
   But by book,
And Thy Book alone.

10

Though I fail, I weep;
Though I halt in pace,
   Yet I creep
To the throne of grace.

Then let wrath remove;
Love will do the deed;
   For with love
Stony hearts will bleed.

20

Love is swift of foot;
Love's a man of war,
   And can shoot,
And can hit from far.

Who can 'scape his bow?
That which wrought on Thee,
   Brought Thee low,
Needs must work on me.

Throw away Thy rod;
Though man frailties hath,   30
    Thou art God:
Throw away Thy wrath.

From *The Temple* (1633)

The Elixir

Teach me, my God and King,
    In all things Thee to see,
And what I do in anything,
    To do it as for Thee.

Not rudely, as a beast,
    To run into an action;
But still to make Thee prepossest,
    And give it his perfection.

A man that looks on glass,
    On it may stay his eye;   10
Or, if he pleaseth, through it pass,
    And then the heav'n espy.

All may of Thee partake:
    Nothing can be so mean,
Which with his tincture (for Thy sake)
    Will not grow bright and clean.

A servant with this clause
    Makes drudgery divine:
Who sweeps a room as for Thy laws,
    Makes that and th'action fine.   20

This is the famous stone
    That turneth all to gold;

F

For that which God doth touch and own
　　Cannot for less be told.
　　　　　　　　From *The Temple* (1633)

Love

Love bade me welcome; yet my soul drew back,
　　Guilty of dust and sin.
But quick-eyed Love, observing me grow slack
　　From my first entrance in,
Drew nearer to me, sweetly questioning,
　　If I lacked anything.

'A guest,' I answered, 'worthy to be here.'
　　Love said, 'You shall be he.'
'I, the unkind, ungrateful? Ah, my dear,
　　I cannot look on Thee.'　　　　　　10
Love took my hand, and smiling did reply,
　　'Who made the eyes but I?'

'Truth, Lord, but I have marred them: let my shame
　　Go where it doth deserve.'
'And know you not,' says Love, 'who bore the blame?'
　　'My dear, then I will serve.'
'You must sit down,' says Love, 'and taste my meat.'
　　So I did sit and eat.
　　　　　　　　From *The Temple* (1633)

THOMAS CAREW

The Spring

Now that the Winter's gone, the earth hath lost
Her snow-white robes, and now no more the frost
Candies the grass, or casts an icy cream
Upon the silver lake or crystal stream:
But the warm sun thaws the benumbed earth,
And makes it tender, gives a sacred birth
To the dead swallow: wakes in hollow tree
The drowsy cuckoo and the humble-bee.
Now do a choir of chirping minstrels bring
In triumph to the world, the youthful Spring.   10
The valleys, hills, and woods in rich array
Welcome the coming of the long'd for May.
Now all things smile: only my Love doth lour;
Nor hath the scalding noonday sun the power
To melt that marble ice, which still doth hold
Her heart congealed, and makes her pity cold.
The ox, which lately did for shelter fly
Into the stall, doth now securely lie
In open fields; and love no more is made
By the fireside, but in the cooler shade   20
Amyntas now doth with his Chloris sleep
Under a sycamore, and all things keep
Time with the season: only she doth carry
June in her eyes, in her heart January.

From *Poems* (1640)

To A. L.: Persuasions to Love

Think not, 'cause men flatt'ring say
You're fresh as April, sweet as May,

Bright as is the morning star,
That you are so; or, though you are,
Be not therefore proud, and deem
All men unworthy your esteem:
For, being so, you lose the pleasure
Of being fair, since that rich treasure
Of rare beauty and sweet feature
Was bestowed on you by Nature   10
To be enjoyed, and 'twere a sin
There to be scarce, where she hath been
So prodigal of her best graces;
Thus common beauties, and mean faces
Shall have more pastime, and enjoy
The sport you lose by being coy.
Did the thing for which I sue
Only concern myself, not you;
Were men so framed as they alone
Reaped all the pleasure, women none,   20
Then had you reason to be scant;
But 'twere a madness not to grant
That which affords (if you consent)
To you, the giver, more content
Than me, the beggar. Oh, then be
Kind to yourself, if not to me.
Starve not yourself, because you may
Thereby make me pine away;
Nor let brittle beauty make
You your wiser thoughts forsake;   30
For that lovely face will fail:
Beauty's sweet, but beauty's frail;
'Tis sooner past, 'tis sooner done
Than summer's rain, or winter's sun;
Most fleeting when it is most dear,
'Tis gone while we but say 'tis here.
These curious locks so aptly twin'd,
Whose every hair a soul doth bind,
Will change their auburn hue, and grow

White and cold as winter's snow.   40
That eye which now is Cupid's nest
Will prove his grave, and all the rest
Will follow; in the cheek, chin, nose,
Nor lily shall be found, nor rose.
And what will then become of all
Those whom now you servants call?
Like swallows, when your summer's done,
They'll fly, and seek some warmer sun.
Then wisely choose one to your friend
Whose love may, when your beauties end,   50
Remain still firm: be provident,
And think, before the summer's spent,
Of following winter; like the ant,
In plenty hoard for time of scant.
Cull out amongst the multitude
Of lovers, that seek to intrude
Into your favour, one that may
Love for an age, not for a day;
One that will quench your youthful fires,
And feed in age your hot desires.   60
For when the storms of time have moved
Waves on that cheek which was belov'd,
When a fair lady's face is pin'd,
And yellow spread, where red once shin'd,
When beauty, youth, and all sweets leave her,
Love may return, but lover never:
And old folks say there are no pains
Like itch of love in aged veins.
O love me then, and now begin it,
Let us not lose this present minute;   70
For time and age will work that wrack
Which time or age shall ne'er call back.
The snake each year fresh skin resumes,
And eagles change their aged plumes;
The faded rose each spring receives
A fresh red tincture on her leaves:

But if your beauties once decay,
You never know a second May.
O, then be wise, and whilst your season
Affords you days for sport, do reason: 80
Spend not in vain your life's short hour,
But crop in time your beauty's flower,
Which will away, and doth together
Both bud and fade, both blow and wither.

From *Poems* (1640)

To my Mistress sitting by a river's side. An Eddy

Mark how yond eddy steals away
From the rude stream into the bay;
There locked up safe, she doth divorce
Her waters from the channel's course,
And scorns the torrent that did bring
Her headlong from her native spring.
Now doth she with her new love play,
Whilst he runs murmuring away.
Mark how she courts the banks, whilst they
As amorously their arms display,   10
To embrace, and clip her silver waves:
See how she strokes their sides, and craves
An entrance there, which they deny;
Whereat she frowns, threat'ning to fly
Home to her stream, and 'gins to swim
Backward, but from the channel's brim,
Smiling, returns into the creek,
With thousand dimples on her cheek.
Be thou this eddy, and I'll make
My breast thy shore, where thou shalt take   20
Secure repose, and never dream
Of the quite forsaken stream:
Let him to the wide ocean haste,

There lose his colour, name and taste:
Thou shalt save all, and safe from him
Within these arms for ever swim.

From *Poems* (1640)

Song. To my Inconstant Mistress

When thou, poor excommunicate
  From all the joys of love, shalt see
The full reward and glorious fate
  Which my strong faith shall purchase me,
  Then curse thine own inconstancy.

A fairer hand than thine shall cure
  That heart, which thy false oaths did wound;
And to my soul, a soul more pure
  Than thine, shall by Love's hand be bound,
  And both with equal glory crowned.   10

Then shalt thou weep, entreat, complain
  To Love, as I did once to thee;
When all thy tears shall be as vain
  As mine were then, for thou shalt be
  Damn'd for thy false apostacy.

From *Poems* (1640)

Disdain Returned

He that loves a rosy cheek,
  Or a coral lip admires,
Or from star-like eyes doth seek
  Fuel to maintain his fires;
As old Time makes these decay,
So his flames must waste away.

But a smooth and steadfast mind,
   Gentle thoughts and calm desires,
Hearts, with equal love combin'd,
   Kindle never-dying fires.   10
Where these are not, I despise
Lovely cheeks, or lips, or eyes.

No tears, Celia, now shall win
   My resolv'd heart to return;
I have search'd thy soul within,
   And find naught but pride and scorn:
I have learn'd thy arts, and now
Can disdain as much as thou.
   Some power, in my revenge, convey
   That love to her I cast away.   20

From *Poems* (1640)

To my Mistress in Absence

Though I must live here, and by force
Of your command suffer divorce;
Though I am parted, yet my mind,
That's more myself, still stays behind.
I breathe in you, you keep my heart;
'Twas but a carcass that did part.
Then though our bodies are disjoined,
As things that are to place confined,
Yet let our boundless spirits meet,
And in love's sphere each other greet;   10
There let us work a mystic wreath,
Unknown unto the world beneath;
There let our clasped loves sweetly twin;
There let our secret thoughts unseen
Like nets be weaved and intertwined,
Wherewith we'll catch each other's mind.

There whilst our souls do sit and kiss,
Tasting a sweet and subtle bliss
(Such as gross lovers cannot know,
Whose hands and lips meet here below),   20
Let us look down, and mark what pain
Our absent bodies here sustain,
And smile to see how far away
The one doth from the other stray;
Yet burn and languish with desire
To join, and quench their mutual fire;
There let us joy to see from far
Our emulous flames at loving war,
Whilst both with equal lustre shine,
Mine bright as yours, yours bright as mine.   30
There seated in those heavenly bowers,
We'll cheat the lag and ling'ring hours,
Making our bitter absence sweet,
Till souls and bodies both may meet.

From *Poems* (1640)

Epitaph on the Lady Mary Villiers

This little vault, this narrow room,
Of love and beauty is the tomb;
The dawning beam that 'gan to clear
Our clouded sky lies dark'ned here,
For ever set to us, by death
Sent to inflame the world beneath.
'Twas but a bud, yet did contain
More sweetness than shall spring again;
A budding star that might have grown
Into a sun when it had blown.   10
This hopeful beauty did create
New life in Love's declining state;
But now his empire ends, and we

From fire and wounding darts are free;
His brand, his bow, let no man fear:
The flames, the arrows, all lie here.

                                        From *Poems* (1640)

To Ben Jonson: Upon the occasion of his Ode of defiance annexed to his Play of 'The New Inn'

'Tis true, dear Ben, thy just chastising hand
Hath fixed upon the sotted age a brand,
To their swoln pride and empty scribbling due;
It can nor judge nor write; and yet 'tis true
Thy comic Muse, from the exalted line
Touch'd by thy *Alchemist*, doth since decline
From that her zenith, and foretells a red
And blushing evening, when she goes to bed;
Yet such as shall outshine the glimmering light
With which all stars shall gild the following night.   10
Nor think it much, since all thy eaglets may
Endure the sunny trial, if we say
This hath the stronger wing, or that doth shine
Trick'd up in fairer plumes, since all are thine.
Who hath his flock of cackling geese compar'd
With thy tun'd choir of swans? or else who dar'd
To call thy births deformed? But if thou bind
By city-custom or by gavel-kind
In equal shares thy love on all thy race,
We may distinguish of their sex and place;   20
Though one hand form them, and though one brain strike
Souls into all, they are not all alike.
Why should the follies, then, of this dull age
Draw from thy pen such an immodest rage,
As seems to blast thy (else-immortal) bays,
When thine own tongue proclaims thy itch of praise?
Such thirst will argue drouth. No, let be hurl'd

Upon thy works by the detracting world
What malice can suggest: let the rout say
The running sands that, ere thou make a play, 30
Count the slow minutes, might a *Goodwin* frame,
To swallow when th'hast done thy shipwracked name.
Let them the dear expense of oil upbraid,
Suck'd by thy watchful lamp, that hath betray'd
To theft the blood of martyred authors, spilt
Into thy ink, whilst thou growest pale with guilt.
Repine not at the taper's thrifty waste,
That sleeks thy terser poems; nor is haste
Praise, but excuse; and if thou overcome
A knotty writer, bring the booty home; 40
Nor think it theft, if the rich spoils so torn
From conquered authors be as trophies worn.
Let others glut on the extorted praise
Of vulgar breath; trust thou to after days:
Thy laboured works shall live, when Time devours
Th'abortive offspring of their hasty hours.
Thou art not of their rank, the quarrel lies
Within thine own verge: then let this suffice,
The wiser world doth greater thee confess
Than all men else, than thyself only less. 50

From *Poems* (1640)

From *An Elegy upon the Death of the Dean of Paul's, Dr. John Donne*

Oh, pardon me, that break with untuned verse
The reverend silence that attend thy hearse,
Whose awful solemn murmurs were to thee,
More than these faint lines, a loud elegy,
That did proclaim in a dumb eloquence
The death of all the arts; whose influence,
Grown feeble, in these panting numbers lies

Gasping short-winded accents, and so dies.
So doth the swiftly turning wheel not stand
In th'instant we withdraw the moving hand,   10
But some small time maintain a faint weak course,
By virtue of the first impulsive force:
And so while I cast on thy funeral pile
Thy crown of bays: Oh, let it crack awile,
And spit disdain, till the devouring flashes
Suck all the moisture up, then turn to ashes.
  I will not draw the envy to engross
All thy perfections, or weep all our loss;
Those are too numerous for an elegy,
And this too great to be expressed by me.   20
Though every pen should share a distinct part,
Yet art thou theme enough to tire all art;
Let others carve the rest: it shall suffice
I on thy tomb this epitaph incise:

  Here lies a King, that rul'd as he thought fit
  The universal monarchy of wit;
  Here lie two flamens, and both those the best,
  Apollo's first, at last, the true God's priest.
                              From *Poems* (1640)

JOHN MILTON

On the Morning of Christ's Nativity

This is the month, and this the happy morn
Wherein the Son of Heaven's eternal King,
Of wedded maid, and virgin mother born,
Our great redemption from above did bring;
For so the holy sages once did sing,
 That He our deadly forfeit should release,
And with His Father work us a perpetual peace.

That glorious Form, that Light unsufferable,
And that far-beaming blaze of Majesty,
Wherewith He wont at Heaven's high council-table,   10
To sit the midst of Trinal Unity,
He laid aside; and here with us to be,
 Forsook the courts of everlasting day,
And chose with us a darksome house of mortal clay.

Say, heavenly Muse, shall not thy sacred vein
Afford a present to the Infant God?
Hast thou no verse, no hymn, or solemn strain,
To welcome Him to this His new abode,
Now while the heaven, by the sun's team untrod,
 Hath took no print of the approaching light,   20
And all the spangled host keep watch in squadrons bright?

See how from far, upon the eastern road,
The star-led wizards haste with odours sweet:
O run, prevent them with thy humble ode,
And lay it lowly at His blessed feet;
Have thou the honour first, thy Lord to greet,
 And join thy voice unto the angel quire,
From out His secret altar touch'd with hallow'd fire.

THE HYMN

It was the winter wild,
While the heaven-born Child,   30
  All meanly wrapt in the rude manger lies;
Nature in awe to Him
Had doff'd her gaudy trim,
  With her great Master so to sympathize:
It was no season then for her
To wanton with the sun, her lusty paramour.

Only with speeches fair
She woos the gentle air
  To hide her guilty front with innocent snow,
And on her naked shame,   40
Pollute with sinful blame,
  The saintly veil of maiden white to throw,
Confounded, that her Maker's eyes
Should look so near upon her foul deformities.

But He, her fears to cease,
Sent down the meek-eyed Peace;
  She, crowned with olive green, came softly sliding
Down through the turning sphere,
His ready harbinger,
  With turtle wing the amorous clouds dividing;   50
And waving wide her myrtle wand,
She strikes a universal peace through sea and land.

No war, or battle's sound
Was heard the world around:
  The idle spear and shield were high up hung;
The hooked chariot stood
Unstained with hostile blood;
  The trumpet spake not to the armed throng;
And kings sat still with awful eye,
As if they surely knew their sovran Lord was by.   60

But peaceful was the night
Wherein the Prince of Light
  His reign of peace upon the earth began:
The winds, with wonder whist,
Smoothly the waters kist,
  Whispering new joys to the mild ocean,
Who now hath quite forgot to rave,
While birds of calm sit brooding on the charmed wave.

The stars, with deep amaze,
Stand fix'd in steadfast gaze,   70
  Bending one way their precious influence;
And will not take their flight
For all the morning light,
  Or Lucifer that often warn'd them thence;
But in their glimmering orbs did glow,
Until their Lord Himself bespake, and bid them go.

And though the shady gloom
Had given day her room,
  The sun himself withheld his wonted speed,
And hid his head for shame,   80
As his inferior flame
  The new-enlightened world no more should need;
He saw a greater Sun appear
Than his bright throne or burning axle tree could bear.

The shepherds on the lawn
Or ere the point of dawn
  Sat simply chatting in a rustic row;
Full little thought they than
That the mighty Pan
  Was kindly come to live with them below;   90
Perhaps their loves, or else their sheep,
Was all that did their silly thoughts so busy keep.

When such music sweet
Their hearts and ears did greet,
   As never was by mortal finger strook,
Divinely-warbled voice
Answering the stringed noise,
   As all their souls in blissful rapture took:
The air, such pleasure loth to lose,
With thousand echoes still prolongs each heavenly close.   100

Nature that heard such sound
Beneath the hollow round
   Of Cynthia's seat the airy region thrilling,
Now was almost won
To think her part was done,
   And that her reign had here its last fulfilling;
She knew such harmony alone
Could hold all heaven and earth in happier union.

At last surrounds their sight
A globe of circular light,   110
   That with long beams the shamefaced night array'd;
The helmed Cherubim
And sworded Seraphim
   Are seen in glittering ranks with wings display'd,
Harping in loud and solemn quire
With unexpressive notes to Heaven's new-born Heir.

Such music (as 'tis said)
Before was never made,
   But when of old the sons of morning sung,
While the Creator great   120
His constellations set,
   And the well-balanced world on hinges hung,
And cast the dark foundations deep,
And bid the weltering waves their oozy channel keep.

Ring out, ye crystal spheres,
Once bless our human ears,

If ye have power to touch our senses so;
And let your silver chime
Move in melodious time;
   And let the base of heaven's deep organ blow,   130
And with your ninefold harmony
Make up full consort to the angelic symphony.

For if such holy song
Enwrap our fancy long,
   Time will run back, and fetch the age of gold;
And speckled vanity
Will sicken soon and die,
   And leprous sin will melt from earthly mould;
And Hell itself will pass away,
And leave her dolorous mansions to the peering day.   140

Yea, Truth and Justice then
Will down return to men,
   Orbed in a rainbow; and, like glories wearing,
Mercy will sit between
Thron'd in celestial sheen,
   With radiant feet the tissued clouds down steering;
And Heaven, as at some festival,
Will open wide the gates of her high palace hall.

But wisest Fate says No,
This must not yet be so;   150
   The Babe lies yet in smiling infancy,
That on the bitter cross
Must redeem our loss;
   So both Himself and us to glorify:
Yet first, to those ychain'd in sleep,
The wakeful trump of doom must thunder through the deep,

With such a horrid clang
As on mount Sinai rang
   While the red fire and smouldering clouds outbrake:

G

The aged Earth aghast   160
With terror of that blast
   Shall from the surface to the centre shake,
When, at the world's last session,
The dreadful Judge in middle air shall spread His throne.

And then at last our bliss
Full and perfect is,
   And now begins; for from this happy day
The old Dragon underground,
In straighter limits bound,
   Not half so far casts his usurped sway,   170
And, wrath to see his kingdom fail,
Swinges the scaly horror of his folded tail.

The oracles are dumb;
No voice or hideous hum
   Runs through the arched roof in words deceiving.
Apollo from his shrine
Can no more divine,
   With hollow shriek the steep of Delphos leaving.
No nightly trance or breathed spell
Inspires the pale-eyed priest from the prophetic cell.   180

The lonely mountains o'er
And the resounding shore,
   A voice of weeping heard, and loud lament;
From haunted spring and dale
Edged with poplar pale
   The parting Genius is with sighing sent;
With flower-inwoven tresses torn
The nymphs in twilight shades of tangled thickets mourn.

In consecrated earth
And on the holy earth   190
   The Lars and Lemures moan with midnight plaint;
In urns and altars round

A drear and dying sound
  Affrights the Flamens at their service quaint;
And the chill marble seems to sweat,
While each peculiar Power forgoes his wonted seat.

Peor and Baalim
Forsake their temples dim,
  With that twice battered god of Palestine;
And mooned Ashtaroth,   200
Heaven's queen and mother both,
  Now sits not girt with tapers' holy shrine;
The Libyc Hammon shrinks his horn,
In vain the Tyrian maids their wounded Thammuz mourn.

And sullen Moloch, fled,
Hath left in shadows dread
  His burning idol all of blackest hue;
In vain with cymbals' ring
They call the grisly king,
  In dismal dance about the furnace blue;   210
The brutish gods of Nile as fast,
Isis and Orus and the dog Anubis haste.

Nor is Osiris seen
In Memphian grove or green
  Trampling the unshower'd grass with lowings loud:
Nor can he be at rest
Within his sacred chest;
  Nought but profoundest hell can be his shroud;
In vain with timbrell'd anthems dark
The sable-stoled sorcerers bear his worshipt ark.   220

He feels from Judah's land
The dreaded Infant's hand;
  The rays of Bethlehem blind his dusky eyn;
Nor all the gods beside
Longer dare abide,

Not Typhon huge ending in snaky twine:
Our Babe, to show His Godhead true,
Can in His swaddling bands control the damned crew.

So when the sun in bed,
Curtained with cloudy red,   230
   Pillows his chin upon an orient wave,
The flocking shadows pale
Troop to the infernal jail,
   Each fettered ghost slips to his several grave;
And the yellow-skirted fays
Fly after the night-steeds, leaving their moon-loved maze.

But see, the Virgin blest
Hath laid her Babe to rest;
   Time is our tedious song should here have ending:
Heaven's youngest teemed star   240
Hath fixed her polished car,
   Her sleeping Lord with handmaid lamp attending;
And all about the courtly stable
Bright-harnessed angels sit in order serviceable.

From *Poems* (1645)

On Time

Fly, envious Time, till thou run out thy race;
Call on the lazy, leaden-stepping hours,
Whose speed is but the heavy plummet's pace;
And glut thyself with what thy womb devours,
Which is no more than what is false and vain,
And merely mortal dross;
So little is our loss,
So little is thy gain.
For when as each thing bad thou hast entomb'd,
And, last of all, thy greedy self consum'd,   10

Then long Eternity shall greet our bliss
With an individual kiss;
And Joy shall overtake us as a flood,
When everything that is sincerely good
And perfectly divine,
With Truth, and Peace, and Love shall ever shine
About the supreme Throne
Of Him, to whose happy-making sight alone,
When once our heavenly-guided soul shall climb,
Then all this earthy grossness quit,   20
Attired with stars, we shall for ever sit
   Triumphing over Death and Chance and thee, O Time.

From *Poems* (1645)

On Shakespeare

What needs my Shakespeare, for his honoured bones,
The labour of an age in piled stones?
Or that his hallowed reliques should be hid
Under a star-ypointing pyramid?
Dear son of memory, great heir of fame,
What need'st thou such weak witness of thy name?
Thou, in our wonder and astonishment,
Hast built thyself a live-long monument.
For whilst to the shame of slow-endeavouring art
Thy easy numbers flow, and that each heart   10
Hath from the leaves of thy unvalu'd book,
Those Delphic lines with deep impression took,
Then thou our fancy of it self bereaving,
Dost make us marble with too much conceiving;
And so sepulchered, in such pomp dost lie,
That kings for such a tomb would wish to die.

From the *Second Folio Edition
of Shakespeare's Works* (1632)

Sonnet

How soon hath Time, the subtle thief of youth,
　　Stol'n on his wing my three and twentieth year!
　　My hasting days fly on with full career,
　　But my late spring no bud or blossom shew'th.
Perhaps my semblance might deceive the truth,
　　That I to manhood am arrived so near,
　　And inward ripeness doth much less appear,
　　That some more timely-happy spirits indu'th.
Yet be it less or more, or soon or slow,
　　It shall be still in strictest measure ev'n,　　　10
　　To that same lot, however mean or high,
Towards which Time leads me, and the will of heav'n;
　　All is, if I have grace to use it so,
　　As ever in my great task Master's eye.

From *Poems* (1645)

At a Solemn Music

Blest pair of Sirens, pledges of Heaven's joy,
Sphere-born harmonious sisters, Voice and Verse!
Wed your divine sounds, and mixt power employ
Dead things with inbreathed sense able to pierce,
And to our high-rais'd phantasy present
That undisturbed song of pure content
Ay sung before the sapphire-colour'd throne
To Him that sits thereon,
With saintly shout, and solemn jubilee;
Where the bright Seraphim in burning row　　　10
Their loud uplifted angel trumpets blow,
And the Cherubic host in thousand quires
Touch their immortal harps of golden wires,
With those just Spirits that wear victorious palms,
Hymns devout and holy psalms

Singing everlastingly;
That we on earth, with undiscording voice,
May rightly answer that melodious noise;
As once we did, till disproportioned sin
Jarred against nature's chime, and with harsh din   20
Broke the fair music that all creatures made
To their great Lord, whose love their motion swayed
In perfect diapason, whilst they stood
In first obedience, and their state of good.
O may we soon again renew that Song,
And keep in tune with Heaven, till God ere long
To His celestial consort us unite,
To live with Him, and sing in endless morn of light.

From *Poems* (1645)

L'Allegro

Hence, loathed Melancholy,
    Of Cerberus and blackest midnight born
In Stygian cave forlorn
    'Mongst horrid shapes, and shrieks, and sights unholy!
Find out some uncouth cell,
    Where brooding Darkness spreads his jealous wings,
And the night-raven sings;
    There, under ebon shades and low-brow'd rocks
As ragged as thy locks,
    In dark Cimmerian desert ever dwell.   10
But come, thou Goddess fair and free,
In heaven yclep'd Euphrosyne,
And, by men, heart-easing mirth,
Whom lovely Venus at a birth
With two sister Graces more
To ivy-crowned Bacchus bore;
Or whether (as some sager sing)
The frolic wind that breathes the spring,

Zephyr, with Aurora playing,
As he met her once a-maying,   20
There, on beds of violets blue
And fresh-blown roses wash'd in dew,
Fill'd her with thee, a daughter fair,
So buxom, blithe, and debonair.
Haste thee, Nymph, and bring with thee
Jest, and youthful jollity,
Quips, and cranks, and wanton wiles,
Nods, and becks, and wreathed smiles,
Such as hang on Hebe's cheek,
And love to live in dimple sleek;   30
Sport that wrinkled Care derides,
And Laughter holding both his sides.
Come, and trip it as you go
On the light fantastic toe;
And in thy right hand lead with thee
The mountain nymph, sweet Liberty;
And if I give thee honour due,
Mirth, admit me of thy crew,
To live with her, and live with thee
In unreproved pleasures free;   40
To hear the lark begin his flight,
And singing startle the dull night
From his watch-tower in the skies,
Till the dappled dawn doth rise;
Then to come, in spite of sorrow,
And at my window bid good morrow,
Through the sweet briar, or the vine,
Or the twisted eglantine:
While the cock with lively din
Scatters the rear of darkness thin,   50
And to the stack, or the barn door,
Stoutly struts his dames before:
Oft listening how the hounds and horn
Cheerly rouse the slumbering morn,
From the side of some hoar hill,

Through the high wood echoing shrill.
Sometimes walking, not unseen,
By hedge-row elms, on hillocks green,
Right against the eastern gate
Where the great sun begins his state,   60
Robed in flames and amber light,
The clouds in thousand liveries dight;
While the ploughman, near at hand,
Whistles o'er the furrowed land,
And the milkmaid singeth blithe,
And the mower whets his scythe,
And every shepherd tells his tale
Under the hawthorn in the dale.
Straight mine eye hath caught new pleasures
Whilst the landscape round it measures;   70
Russet lawns, and fallows grey,
Where the nibbling flocks do stray;
Mountains on whose barren breast
The labouring clouds do often rest;
Meadows trim with daisies pied,
Shallow brooks, and rivers wide;
Towers and battlements it sees
Bosom'd high in tufted trees,
Where, perhaps, some beauty lies,
The Cynosure of neighbouring eyes.   80
Hard by, a cottage chimney smokes
From betwixt two aged oaks,
Where Corydon and Thyrsis, met,
Are at their savoury dinner set
Of herbs, and other country messes
Which the neat-handed Phyllis dresses;
And then in haste her bower she leaves
With Thestylis to bind the sheaves;
Or, if the earlier season lead,
To the tann'd haycock in the mead.   90
Sometimes with secure delight
The upland hamlets will invite,

When the merry bells ring round,
And the jocund rebecks sound
To many a youth and many a maid,
Dancing in the chequered shade;
And young and old come forth to play
On a sunshine holy-day,
Till the live-long daylight fail;
Then to the spicy nut-brown ale,   100
With stories told of many a feat,
How Faery Mab the junkets eat;
She was pinched and pulled, she said;
And he by Friar's lantern led
Tells how the drudging Goblin sweat
To earn his cream-bowl duly set,
When in one night, ere glimpse of morn,
His shadowy flail hath thresh'd the corn
That ten day-labourers could not end;
Then lies him down, the lubber fiend,   110
And, stretch'd out all the chimney's length,
Basks at the fire his hairy strength;
And crop-full out of doors he flings,
Ere the first cock his matin rings.
Thus done the tales, to bed they creep,
By whispering winds soon lulled asleep.
Towered cities please us then,
And the busy hum of men,
Where throngs of knights and barons bold,
In weeds of peace high triumphs hold,   120
With store of ladies, whose bright eyes
Rain influence, and judge the prize
Of wit or arms, while both contend
To win her grace, whom all commend.
There let Hymen oft appear
In saffron robe, with taper clear,
And pomp, and feast, and revelry,
With mask, and antique pageantry,
Such sights as youthful poets dream

On summer eves by haunted stream.   130
Then to the well-trod stage anon,
If Jonson's learned sock be on,
Or sweetest Shakespeare, Fancy's child,
Warble his native wood-notes wild.
And ever against eating cares
Lap me in soft Lydian airs
Married to immortal verse,
Such as the meeting soul may pierce
In notes, with many a winding bout
Of linked sweetness long drawn out,   140
With wanton heed and giddy cunning,
The melting voice through mazes running,
Untwisting all the chains that tie
The hidden soul of harmony;
That Orpheus' self may heave his head
From golden slumber, on a bed
Of heap'd Elysian flowers, and hear
Such strains as would have won the ear
Of Pluto, to have quite set free
His half-regain'd Eurydice.   150
These delights, if thou canst give,
Mirth, with thee I mean to live.

From *Poems* (1645)

Il Penseroso

Hence, vain deluding Joys,
    The brood of Folly without father bred!
How little you bestead
    Or fill the fixed mind with all your toys!
Dwell in some idle brain,
    And fancies fond with gaudy shapes possess
As thick and numberless
    As the gay motes that people the sunbeams,

Or likest hovering dreams
   The fickle pensioners of Morpheus' train.   10
But hail, thou goddess sage and holy,
Hail, divinest Melancholy!
Whose saintly visage is too bright
To hit the sense of human sight,
And therefore to our weaker view
O'erlaid with black, staid Wisdom's hue;
Black, but such as in esteem
Prince Memnon's sister might beseem,
Or that starr'd Ethiop queen that strove
To set her beauty's praise above   20
The sea-nymphs, and their powers offended.
Yet thou art higher far descended:
Thee bright-haired Vesta, long of yore,
To solitary Saturn bore;
His daughter she, (in Saturn's reign
Such mixture was not held a stain),
Oft in glimmering bowers and glades
He met her, and in secret shades
Of woody Ida's inmost grove,
While yet there was no fear of Jove.   30
Come, pensive nun, devout and pure,
Sober, steadfast, and demure,
All in a robe of darkest grain
Flowing with majestic train,
And sable stole of cypres lawn
Over thy decent shoulders drawn.
Come, but keep thy wonted state,
With even step, and musing gait,
And looks commercing with the skies,
Thy rapt soul sitting in thine eyes: 40
There, held in holy passion still,
Forget thyself to marble, till
With a sad leaden downward cast
Thou fix them on the earth as fast.
And join with thee calm Peace, and Quiet,

Spare Fast, that oft with gods doth diet,
And hears the Muses in a ring
Ay round about Jove's altar sing.
And add to these retired Leisure
That in trim gardens takes his pleasure;   50
But first, and chiefest, with thee bring
Him that yon soars on golden wing,
Guiding the fiery-wheeled throne,
The cherub Contemplation;
And the mute silence hist along,
'Less Philomel will deign a song
In her sweetest, saddest plight,
Smoothing the rugged brow of Night,
While Cynthia checks her dragon yoke
Gently o'er the accustomed oak.   60
Sweet bird, that shunn'st the noise of folly,
Most musical, most melancholy!
Thee, chauntress, oft, the woods among
I woo, to hear thy evensong;
And missing thee, I walk unseen
On the dry, smooth-shaven green,
To behold the wandering moon
Riding near her highest noon,
Like one that had been led astray
Through the heaven's wide pathless way;   70
And oft, as if her head she bowed,
Stooping through a fleecy cloud.
Oft on a plat of rising ground
I hear the far-off curfew sound
Over some wide-watered shore,
Swinging slow with sullen roar;
Or, if the air will not permit,
Some still removed place will fit,
Where glowing embers through the room
Teach light to counterfeit a gloom;   80
Far from all resort of mirth,
Save the cricket on the hearth,

Or the bellman's drowsy charm
To bless the doors from nightly harm;
Or let my lamp at midnight hour
Be seen in some high lonely tower,
Where I may oft out-watch the Bear
With thrice-great Hermes, or unsphere
The spirit of Plato, to unfold
What worlds or what vast regions hold   90
The immortal mind that hath forsook
Her mansion in this fleshly nook:
And of those dæmons that are found
In fire, air, flood, or underground,
Whose power hath a true consent
With planet, or with element.
Sometime let gorgeous Tragedy
In sceptered pall come sweeping by,
Presenting Thebes, or Pelops' line,
Or the tale of Troy divine;   100
Or what (though rare) of later age
Ennobled hath the buskined stage.
But, O sad Virgin, that thy power
Might raise Musæus from his bower,
Or bid the soul of Orpheus sing
Such notes as, warbled to the string,
Drew iron tears down Pluto's cheek,
And made Hell grant what Love did seek.
Or call up him that left half-told
The story of Cambuscan bold,   110
Of Camball, and of Algarsife,
And who had Canace to wife,
That owned the virtuous ring and glass,
And of the wondrous horse of brass,
On which the Tartar king did ride;
And if aught else great bards beside
In sage and solemn tunes have sung
Of turneys, and of trophies hung,
Of forests and enchantments drear,

Where more is meant than meets the ear.   120
Thus, Night, oft see me in thy pale career,
Till civil-suited Morn appear,
Not trick'd and frounced as she was wont
With the Attic Boy to hunt,
But kercheft in a comely cloud
While rocking winds are piping loud,
Or ushered with a shower still,
When the gust hath blown his fill,
Ending on the rustling leaves
With minute drops from off the eaves.   130
And when the sun begins to fling
His flaring beams, me, goddess, bring
To arched walks of twilight groves,
And shadows brown, that Sylvan loves,
Of pine, or monumental oak,
Where the rude axe, with heaved stroke,
Was never heard the nymphs to daunt,
Or fright them from their hallowed haunt.
There in close covert by some brook
Where no profaner eye may look,   140
Hide me from day's garish eye,
While the bee with honey'd thigh,
That at her flowery work doth sing,
And the waters murmuring,
With such consort as they keep
Entice the dewy-feathered Sleep;
And let some strange mysterious dream
Wave at his wings in airy stream
Of lively portraiture displayed,
Softly on my eyelids laid.   150
And, as I wake, sweet music breathe
Above, about, or underneath,
Sent by some spirit to mortals good,
Or the unseen Genius of the wood.
But let my due feet never fail
To walk the studious cloister's pale,

And love the high-embowed roof,
With antique pillars massy-proof,
And storied windows richly dight,
Casting a dim religious light.   160
There let the pealing organ blow
To the full-voiced quire below
In service high and anthems clear,
As may with sweetness, through mine ear,
Dissolve me into ecstasies,
And bring all heaven before mine eyes.
And may at last my weary age
Find out the peaceful hermitage,
The hairy gown and mossy cell
Where I may sit and rightly spell   170
Of every star that heaven doth show,
And every herb that sips the dew;
Till old experience do attain
To something like prophetic strain.
These pleasures, Melancholy, give,
And I with thee will choose to live.

From *Poems* (1645)

'*Sweet Echo, sweetest Nymph*'

Sweet Echo, sweetest Nymph that liv'st unseen
          Within thy airy shell,
      By slow Meander's margent green,
And in the violet-embroider'd vale
      Where the love-lorn Nightingale
Nightly to thee her sad song mourneth well.
Canst thou not tell me of a gentle Pair
          That likest thy Narcissus are?
              O if thou have
          Hid them in some flowery cave,   10
              Tell me but where,

Sweet Queen of Parly, Daughter of the Sphere,
So may'st thou be translated to the skies,
And give resounding grace to all heaven's harmonies.
                        From *Comus. A Masque presented at*
                                      Ludlow Castle (1634)

Lycidas

Yet once more, O ye laurels, and once more
Ye myrtles brown, with ivy never sere,
I come to pluck your berries harsh and crude,
And with forced fingers rude
Shatter your leaves before the mellowing year.
Bitter constraint, and sad occasion dear,
Compels me to disturb your season due:
For Lycidas is dead, dead ere his prime,
Young Lycidas, and hath not left his peer:
Who would not sing for Lycidas? he knew   10
Himself to sing, and build the lofty rhyme.
He must not float upon his watery bier
Unwept, and welter to the parching wind,
Without the meed of some melodious tear.
    Begin then, Sisters of the sacred well
That from beneath the seat of Jove doth spring,
Begin, and somewhat loudly sweep the string.
Hence with denial vain and coy excuse;
So may some gentle Muse
With lucky words favour my destined urn;   20
And as he passes, turn
And bid fair peace be to my sable shroud.
    For we were nursed upon the self-same hill,
Fed the same flock by fountain, shade, and rill.
Together both, ere the high lawns appeared
Under the opening eye-lids of the morn,
We drove a-field, and both together heard

H

What time the gray-fly winds her sultry horn,
Battening our flocks with the fresh dews of night,
Oft till the star, that rose at evening bright,   30
Toward heaven's descent had sloped his westering wheel.
Meanwhile the rural ditties were not mute,
Temper'd to the oaten flute;
Rough Satyrs danced, and Fauns with cloven heel
From the glad sound would not be absent long;
And old Damœtas loved to hear our song.

But O the heavy change, now thou art gone,
Now thou art gone, and never must return!
Thee, Shepherd, thee the woods and desert caves,
With wild thyme and the gadding vine o'ergrown,   40
And all their echoes mourn.
The willows and the hazel copses green
Shall now no more be seen
Fanning their joyous leaves to thy soft lays.
As killing as the canker to the rose,
Or taint-worm to the weanling herds that graze,
Or frost to flowers, that their gay wardrobe wear,
When first the white-thorn blows;
Such, Lycidas, thy loss to shepherd's ear.

Where were ye, Nymphs, when the remorseless deep 50
Closed o'er the head of your loved Lycidas?
For neither were ye playing on the steep
Where your old bards, the famous Druids, lie,
Nor on the shaggy top of Mona high,
Nor yet where Deva spreads her wizard stream:
Ay me, I fondly dream!
Had ye been there, for what could that have done?
What could the Muse herself that Orpheus bore,
The Muse herself, for her enchanting son,
Whom universal nature did lament,   60
When by the rout that made the hideous roar
His gory visage down the stream was sent,
Down the swift Hebrus to the Lesbian shore?

Alas! what boots it with uncessant care

To tend the homely, slighted shepherd's trade,
And strictly meditate the thankless Muse?
Were it not better done, as others use,
To sport with Amaryllis in the shade,
Or with the tangles of Neæra's hair?
Fame is the spur that the clear spirit doth raise   70
(That last infirmity of noble mind)
To scorn delights, and live laborious days;
But the fair guerdon when we hope to find
And think to burst out into sudden blaze,
Comes the blind Fury with the abhorred shears
And slits the thin-spun life. 'But not the praise',
Phoebus replied, and touched my trembling ears;
'Fame is no plant that grows on mortal soil,
Nor in the glistering foil
Set off to the world, nor in broad rumour lies;   80
But lives and spreads aloft by those pure eyes
And perfect witness of all-judging Jove;
As he pronounces lastly on each deed,
Of so much fame in heaven expect thy meed.'

   O fountain Arethuse, and thou honour'd flood,
Smooth-sliding Mincius, crown'd with vocal reeds,
That strain I heard was of a higher mood:
But now my oat proceeds,
And listens to the herald of the sea
That came in Neptune's plea;   90
He asked the waves, and asked the felon winds,
What hard mishap hath doom'd this gentle swain?
And question'd every gust of rugged wings
That blows from off each beaked promontory:
They knew not of his story;
And sage Hippotades their answer brings,
That not a blast was from his dungeon strayed;
The air was calm, and on the level brine
Sleek Panope with all her sisters played.
It was that fatal and perfidious bark   100
Built in the eclipse, and rigged with curses dark,

That sunk so low that sacred head of thine.
    Next Camus, reverend sire, went footing slow,
His mantle hairy, and his bonnet sedge,
Inwrought with figures dim, and on the edge
Like to that sanguine flower inscribed with woe.
'Ah! who hath reft,' quoth he, 'my dearest pledge?'
Last came, and last did go,
The Pilot of the Galilean lake;
Two massy keys he bore of metals twain   110
(The golden opes, the iron shuts amain);
He shook his mitred locks, and stern bespake:
'How well could I have spared for thee, young swain,
Enow of such as for their bellies' sake
Creep and intrude and climb into the fold!
Of other care they little reckoning make
Than how to scramble at the shearer's feast,
And shove away the worthy bidden guest.
Blind mouths! that scarce themselves know how to hold
A sheep-hook, or have learn'd aught else the least   120
That to the faithful herdman's art belongs!
What recks it them? What need they? They are sped;
And when they list, their lean and flashy songs
Grate on their scrannel pipes of wretched straw;
The hungry sheep look up, and are not fed,
But swoln with wind and the rank mist they draw
Rot inwardly, and foul contagion spread;
Besides what the grim wolf with privy paw
Daily devours apace, and nothing said;
But that two-handed engine at the door   130
Stands ready to smite once, and smite no more.'
    Return, Alpheus, the dread voice is past
That shrunk thy streams; return, Sicilian Muse,
And call the vales, and bid them hither cast
Their bells and flow'rets of a thousand hues.
Ye valleys low, where the mild whispers use
Of shades, and wanton winds, and gushing brooks,
On whose fresh lap the swart star sparely looks,

Throw hither all your quaint enamelled eyes
That on the green turf suck the honeyed showers   140
And purple all the ground with vernal flowers.
Bring the rathe primrose that forsaken dies,
The tufted crow-toe, and pale jessamine,
The white pink, and the pansy freaked with jet,
The glowing violet,
The musk-rose, and the well-attired woodbine,
With cowslips wan that hang the pensive head,
And every flower that sad embroidery wears:
Bid Amaranthus all his beauty shed,
And daffadillies fill their cups with tears   150
To strew the laureat hearse where Lycid lies.
For, so to interpose a little ease,
Let our frail thoughts dally with false surmise.
Ay me! Whilst thee the shores and sounding seas
Wash far away, where ere thy bones are hurled,
Whether beyond the stormy Hebrides,
Where thou perhaps, under the whelming tide,
Visitest the bottom of the monstrous world;
Or whether thou, to our moist vows denied,
Sleep'st by the fable of Bellerus old,   160
Where the great vision of the guarded Mount
Looks towards Namancos and Bayona's hold;
Look homeward, Angel, now, and melt with ruth.
And, O ye dolphins, waft the hapless youth!
   Weep no more, woeful shepherds, weep no more,
For Lycidas, your sorrow, is not dead,
Sunk though he be beneath the watery floor;
So sinks the day-star in the ocean-bed,
And yet anon repairs his drooping head
And tricks his beams, and with new-spangled ore   170
Flames in the forehead of the morning sky:
So Lycidas sunk low, but mounted high
Through the dear might of Him that walked the waves;
Where, other groves and other streams along,
With nectar pure his oozy locks he laves,

And hears the unexpressive nuptial song
In the blest kingdoms meek of joy and love.
There entertain him all the saints above
In solemn troops, and sweet societies,
That sing, and singing in their glory move,   180
And wipe the tears for ever from his eyes.
Now, Lycidas, the shepherds weep no more,
Henceforth thou art the Genius of the shore,
In thy large recompense, and shalt be good
To all that wander in that perilous flood.

    Thus sang the uncouth swain to the oaks and rills,
While the still morn went out with sandals grey;
He touch'd the tender stops of various quills,
With eager thought warbling his Doric lay:
And now the sun had stretched out all the hills,   190
And now was dropt into the western bay;
At last he rose, and twitched his mantle blue:
To-morrow to fresh woods, and pastures new.

      From *Justa Edouardo King naufrago* . . . etc. (1638)

On the late Massacre in Piedmont

Avenge, O Lord, Thy slaughtered saints, whose bones
  Lie scattered on the Alpine mountains cold;
  Ev'n them who kept Thy truth so pure of old,
  When all our fathers worship stocks and stones,
Forget not: in Thy book record their groans
  Who were Thy sheep, and in their ancient fold
  Slain by the bloody Piedmontese, that rolled
  Mother with infant down the rocks. Their moans
The vales redoubled to the hills, and they
  To Heaven. Their martyred blood and ashes sow   10
  O'er all the Italian fields, where still doth sway
The triple Tyrant: that from these may grow
  A hundred-fold, who, having learnt Thy way,
  Early may fly the Babylonian woe.

From Poems (1673)

On his Blindness

When I consider how my light is spent,
  Ere half my days, in this dark world and wide,
  And that one talent which is death to hide
  Lodged with me useless, though my soul more bent
To serve therewith my Maker, and present
  My true account, lest He returning chide,
  'Doth God exact day-labour, light denied?'
  I fondly ask; but Patience, to prevent
That murmur, soon replies, 'God doth not need
  Either man's work, or His own gifts: who best   10
  Bear His mild yoke, they serve Him best: His state
Is kingly. Thousands at His bidding speed
  And post o'er land and ocean without rest:
  They also serve who only stand and wait.'

From Poems (1673)

SIR JOHN SUCKLING

A Ballad upon a Wedding

I tell thee, Dick, where I have been,
Where I the rarest things have seen,
    Oh, things without compare!
Such sights again cannot be found
In any place on English ground,
    Be it at wake, or fair.

At Charing Cross, hard by the way
Where we, thou know'st, do sell our hay
    There is a house with stairs;
And there did I see coming down
Such folk as are not in our town,
    Forty at least, in pairs.

Amongst the rest, one pest'lent fine
(His beard no bigger, though, than thine)
    Walked on before the rest:
Our landlord looks like nothing to him;
The King (God bless him) 'twould undo him,
    Should he go still so dressed.

At course-a-park, without all doubt,
He should have first been taken out
    By all the maids i'th' town,
Though lusty Roger there had been,
Or little George upon the Green,
    Or Vincent of the Crown.

But wot you what? the youth was going
To make an end of all his wooing;
    The parson for him stay'd:
Yet by his leave, for all his haste,

He did not so much wish all past,
        Perchance, as did the maid.   30

The maid (and thereby hangs a tale)
For such a maid no Whitsun-ale
        Could ever yet produce:
No grape that's kindly ripe could be
So round, so plump, so soft as she,
        Nor half so full of juice.

Her finger was so small, the ring
Would not stay on, which they did bring,
        It was too wide a peck;
And to say truth (for out it must)   40
It looked like the great collar (just)
        About our young colt's neck.

Her feet beneath her petticoat
Like little mice stole in and out,
        As if they feared the light;
But oh! she dances such a way,
No sun upon an Easter day
        Is half so fine a sight.

He would have kiss'd her once or twice,
But she would not, she was so nice,   50
        She would not do't in sight;
And then she looked as who should say,
'I will do what I list to-day,
        And you shall do't at night.'

Her cheeks so rare a white was on,
No daisy makes comparison,
        (Who sees them is undone);
For streaks of red were mingled there,
Such as are on a Katherine pear,
        (The side that's next the sun).   60

Her lips were red, and one was thin,
Compar'd to that was next her chin:
        (Some bee had stung it newly);
But, Dick, her eyes so guard her face,
I durst no more upon them gaze
        Than on the sun in July.

Her mouth so small, when she does speak,
Thou'dst swear her teeth her words did break,
        That they might passage get;
But she so handled still the matter,   70
They came as good as ours, or better,
        And are not spent a whit.

If wishing should be any sin,
The parson himself had guilty bin,
        (She look'd that day so purely);
And, did the youth so oft the feat
At night, as some did in conceit,
        It would have spoil'd him surely.

Just in the nick the cook knocked thrice,
And all the waiters in a trice   80
        His summons did obey;
Each serving-man, with dish in hand,
Marched boldly up, like our trained band,
        Presented, and away.

When all the meat was on the table,
What man, of knife, or teeth was able
        To stay to be entreated!
And this the very reason was,
Before the parson could say grace,
        The company was seated.   90

The business of the kitchen's great,
For it is fit that men should eat;

Nor was it there denied:
Passion o'me, how I run on!
There's that that would be thought upon
        (I trow) besides the bride.

Now hats fly off, and youths carouse;
Healths first go round, and then the house,
        The bride's came thick and thick:
And when 'twas named another's health,   100
Perhaps he made it hers by stealth:
        (And who could help it, Dick?)

O' th' sudden up they rise and dance;
Then sit again, and sigh, and glance:
        Then dance again and kiss;
Thus several ways the time did pass,
Whilst ev'ry woman wished her place,
        And ev'ry man wished his.

By this time all were stol'n aside
To counsel and undress the bride;   110
        But that he must not know:
But yet 'twas thought he guessed her mind,
And did not mean to stay behind
        Above an hour or so.

When in he came, Dick, there she lay
Like new-fall'n snow melting away
        ('Twas time, I trow, to part);
Kisses were now the only stay,
Which soon she gave, as who would say,
        'God b'w'ye, with all my heart.'   120

But, just as heav'ns would have, to cross it,
In came the bridesmaids with the posset:
        The bridegroom ate in spite;
For had he left the women to't,

It would have cost two hours to do't,
     Which were too much that night.

At length the candle's out, and out,
All that they had not done they do't:
     What that is, who can tell?
But I believe it was no more   130
Than thou and I have done before
     With Bridget, and with Nell.
          From *Fragmenta Aurea* (1646)

Sonnet I '*Of thee, kind boy*'

Of thee, kind boy, I ask no red and white,
     To make up my delight:
     No odd becoming graces,
Black eyes, or little know-not-whats in faces;
Make me but mad enough, give me good store
Of love for her I court:
     I ask no more,
'Tis love in love that makes the sport.

There's no such thing as that we beauty call,
     It is mere cozenage all;   10
     For though some long ago
Liked certain colours mingled so and so,
That doth not tie me now from choosing new.
If I a fancy take
     To black and blue,
That fancy doth it beauty make.

'Tis not the meat, but 'tis the appetite
     Makes eating a delight,
     And if I like one dish
More than another, that a pheasant is;   20

What in our watches, that in us is found;
So to the height and nick
      We up be wound,
No matter by what hand or trick.

Sonnet II *'O for some honest lover's ghost'*

O for some honest lover's ghost,
      Some kind unbodied post
      Sent from the shades below!
      I strangely long to know
Whether the nobler chaplets wear,
Those that their mistress' scorn did bear,
      Or those that were used kindly.

For whatso'er they tell us here
      To make those sufferings dear,
      'Twill there, I fear, be found   10
      That to the being crown'd
T'have loved alone will not suffice,
Unless we also have been wise,
      And have our loves enjoyed.

What posture can we think him in,
      That here unlov'd agen
      Departs, and 's thither gone,
      Where each sits by his own?
Or how can that Elysium be,
Where I my mistress still must see   20
      Circled in others' arms?

For there the judges all are just,
      And Sophonisba must
      Be his whom she held dear,
      Not his who lov'd her here.

The sweet Philoclea, since she died,
Lies by her Pyrocles his side,
      Not by Amphialus.

Some bays, perchance, or myrtle bough,
      For difference crowns the brow   30
          Of those kind souls that were
          The noble martyrs here;
And if that be the only odds
(As who can tell?), ye kinder gods,
          Give me the woman here.
              From *Fragmenta Aurea* (1646)

'Why so pale and wan?'

Why so pale and wan, fond lover?
      Prithee, why so pale?
Will, when looking well can't move her,
      Looking ill prevail?
      Prithee, why so pale?

Why so dull and mute, young sinner?
      Prithee, why so mute?
Will, when speaking well can't win her,
      Saying nothing do't?
      Prithee, why so mute?   10

Quit, quit for shame; this will not move,
      This cannot take her;
If of herself she will not love,
      Nothing can make her:
      The devil take her!
              From *Aglaura*, IV. ii. 15–29 (1646)

Against Fruition

Stay here, fond youth, and ask no more, be wise,
Knowing too much long since lost paradise.
The virtuous joys thou hast, thou wouldst should still
Last in their pride; and wouldst not take it ill,
If rudely from sweet dreams (and for a toy)
Thou wert waked? he wakes himself, that does enjoy.

Fruition adds no new wealth, but destroys,
And while it pleaseth much the palate, cloys;
Who thinks he shall be happier for that,
As reasonably might hope he might grow fat   10
By eating to a surfeit; this once past,
What relishes? even kisses lose their taste.

Urge not 'tis necessary: alas! we know
The homeliest thing which mankind does is so;
The world is of a vast extent, we see,
And must be peopled; children there must be;
So must bread too; but since they are enough
Born to the drudgery, what need we plough?

Women enjoyed (whate'er before they've been)
Are like romances read, or sights once seen;   20
Fruition's dull, and spoils the play much more
Than if one read, or knew the plot before;
'Tis expectation makes a blessing dear,
Heaven were not heaven, if we knew what it were.

And as in prospects we are there pleased most,
Where something keeps the eye from being lost,
And leaves us room to guess, so here restraint
Holds up delight, that with excess would faint.
They who know all the wealth they have are poor;
He's only rich that cannot tell his store.   30

From *Fragmenta Aurea* (1646)

*Upon My Lady Carlisle Walking in Hampton Court
Garden*

Dialogue

T.C.   J.S.

Tom: Didst thou not find the place inspired,
And flowers, as if they had desired
No other sun, start from their beds,
And for a sight steal out their heads?
Heard'st thou not music when she talked?
And didst not find that as she walked
She threw rare perfumes all about,
Such as bean-blossoms newly out,
Or chafed spices give?

J.S.: I must confess those perfumes, Tom,   10
I did not smell; nor found that from
Her passing by aught sprang up new;
The flowers had all their birth from you;
For I passed o'er the self same walk,
And did not find one single stalk
Of any thing that was to bring
This unknown after-after Spring.

Tom: Dull and insensible, could'st see
A thing so near a Deity
Move up and down, and feel no change?   20

J.S.: None, and so great, were alike strange.
I had my thoughts, but not your way;
All are not born, sir, to the bay;
Alas! Tom, I am flesh and blood,
And was consulting how I could
In spite of masks and hoods descry
The parts denied unto the eye:
I was undoing all she wore;
And had she walked but one turn more,

Eve in her first state had not been   30
More naked, or more plainly seen.

Tom: 'Twas well for thee she left the place;
There is great danger in that face;
But hadst thou viewed her leg and thigh,
And upon that discovery
Searched after parts that are more dear
(As fancy seldom stops so near),
No time or age had ever seen
So lost a thing as thou hadst been.

From *Fragmenta Aurea* (1646)

Love turned to Hatred

I will not love one minute more, I swear,
No, not a minute; not a sigh or tear
Thou gett'st from me, or one kind look agen,
Though thou shouldst court me to't and wouldst begin.
I will not think of thee, but as men do
Of debts and sins, and then I'll curse thee too:
For thy sake woman shall be now to me
Less welcome than at midnight ghosts shall be:
I'll hate so perfectly, that it shall be
Treason to love that man that loves a she;   10
Nay, I will hate the very good, I swear,
That's in thy sex, because it doth lie there;
Their very virtue, grace, discourse, and wit,
And all for thee—what, wilt thou love me yet?

From *Fragmenta Aurea* (1646)

Song

I prithee send me back my heart,
  Since I cannot have thine:
For if from yours you will not part,
  Why then shouldst thou have mine?

Yet now I think on't, let it lie:
  To find it were in vain,
For th'hast a thief in either eye
  Would steal it back again.

Why should two hearts in one breast lie,
  And yet not lodge together?   10
O love, where is thy sympathy,
  If thus our breasts thou sever?

But love is such a mystery,
  I cannot find it out:
For when I think I'm best resolved,
  I then am in most doubt.

Then farewell care, and farewell woe,
  I will no longer pine:
For I'll believe I have her heart
  As much as she hath mine.   20

From *Fragmenta Aurea* (1646)

RICHARD CRASHAW

Wishes to his (Supposed) Mistress

Whoe'er she be,
That not impossible She
That shall command my heart and me:

Where'er she lie,
Locked up from mortal eye,
In shady leaves of destiny:

Till that ripe Birth
Of studied Fate stand forth,
And teach her fair steps tread our earth:

Till that divine   10
Idea take a shrine
Of crystal flesh, through which to shine:

Meet you her, my Wishes,
Bespeak her to my blisses,
And be ye called my absent kisses.

I wish her Beauty,
That owes not all his duty
To gaudy tire, or glist'ring shoe-tie:

Something more than
Taffeta or tissue can,   20
Or rampant feather, or rich fan;

More than the spoil
Of shop, or silkworm's toil,
Or a bought blush, or a set smile;

A Face that's best
By its own beauty dressed,
And can alone commend the rest:

A Face made up
Out of no other shop
Than what Nature's white hand sets ope;   30

A Cheek, where youth
And blood, with pen of truth
Write what the reader sweetly ru'th:

A Cheek, where grows
More than a morning rose,
Which to no box its being owes;

Lips, where all day
A lover's kiss may play,
Yet carry nothing thence away;

Looks that oppress   40
Their richest tires, but dress
And clothe their simplest nakedness;

Eyes, that displace
The neighbour diamond, and outface
That sunshine by their own sweet grace;

Tresses, that wear
Jewels, but to declare
How much themselves more precious are,

Whose native ray
Can tame the wanton day   50
Of gems that in their bright shades play.

Each ruby there,
Or pearl that dare appear,
Be its own blush, be its own tear;

A well-tamed Heart,
For whose more noble smart
Love may be long choosing a dart;

Eyes, that bestow
Full quivers on Love's bow,
Yet pay less arrows than they owe;   60

Smiles that can warm
The blood, yet teach a charm
That chastity shall take no harm;

Blushes, that bin
The burnish of no sin,
Nor flames of aught too hot within;

Joys, that confess
Virtue their Mistress,
And have no other head to dress;

Fears fond, and flight,   70
As the coy bride's, when night
First does the longing lover right;

Tears, quickly fled,
And vain, as those are shed
For a dying maidenhead;

Days, that need borrow
No part of their good morrow
From a fore-spent night of sorrow:

Days, that in spite
Of darkness, by the light   80
Of a clear mind are day all night;

Nights, sweet as they,
Made short by lovers' play,
Yet long by the absence of the day;

Life, that dares send
A challenge to his end,
And when it comes say, 'Welcome, friend!'

Sydnæan showers
Of sweet discourse, whose powers
Can crown old Winter's head with flowers;   90

Soft, silken hours,
Open suns, shady bowers,
'Bove all, nothing within that lours.

Whate'er delight
Can make Day's forehead bright,
Or give down to the wings of Night.

In her whole frame
Have Nature all the name,
Art and Ornament the shame!

Her flattery   100
Picture and Poesy:
Her counsel her own virtue be.

I wish her store
Of worth may leave her poor
Of wishes; and I wish—no more.

Now if Time knows
That Her, whose radiant brows
Weave them a garland of my vows,

Her, whose just bays
My future hopes can raise   110
A trophy to her present praise,

Her that dares be
What these lines wish to see:
I seek no further: it is She.

'Tis She, and here
Lo! I unclothe and clear
My Wishes' cloudy character.

May she enjoy it
Whose merit dare apply it,
But modesty dares still deny it!   120

Such worth as this is
Shall fix my flying wishes
And determine them to kisses.

Let her full glory,
My fancies, fly before ye;
Be ye my fictions; but her story.
                    From *The Delights of the Muses* (1646)

From *The Flaming Heart: Upon the Book and
      Picture of the Seraphical Saint Theresa*

O sweet incendiary! show here thy art,
Upon this carcass of a hard, cold heart;
Let all thy scatter'd shafts of light, that play

Among the leaves of thy large books of day,
Combined against this breast, at once break in,
And take away from me myself and sin;
This gracious robbery shall thy bounty be,
And my best fortunes such fair spoils of me.
O thou undaunted daughter of desires!
By all thy dower of lights and fires;   10
By all the eagle in thee, all the dove,
By all thy lives and deaths of love;
By thy large draughts of intellectual day,
And by thy thirsts of love more large than they;
By all thy brim-filled bowls of fierce desire,
By thy last morning's draught of liquid fire;
By the full kingdom of that final kiss
That seized thy parting soul, and sealed thee His;
By all the heav'ns thou hast in Him
(Fair sister of the Seraphim!)   20
By all of Him we have in thee;
Leave nothing of myself in me.
Let me so read thy life, that I
Unto all life of mine may die.

       From *Carmen Deo Nostro* II. 85–108 (1652)

To the Noblest and Best of Ladies, the Countess of Denbigh, Persuading her to Resolution in Religion

What heav'n entreated heart is this,
Stands trembling at the gate of bliss?
Holds fast the door, yet dares not venture
Fairly to open it, and enter:
Whose definition is a doubt
'Twixt life and death, 'twixt in and out?
Say, ling'ring Fair! why comes the birth
Of your brave soul so slowly forth?
Plead your pretences (O you strong

In weakness!) why you choose so long 10
In labour of yourself to lie
Nor daring quite to live nor die.
Ah, linger not, loved soul! a slow
And late consent was a long No;
Who grants at last, a long time tried
And did his best to have denied,
What magic bolts, what mystic bars
Maintain the will in these strange wars?
What fatal, yet fantastic bands
Keep the free heart from its own hands? 20
So when the year takes cold, we see
Poor waters their own prisoners be.
Fettered, and locked up fast they lie
In a sad self-captivity.
The astonished nymphs their flood's strange fate deplore,
To see themselves their own severer shore.
Thou that alone canst thaw this cold
And fetch the heart from its stronghold,
Almighty Love! end this long war,
And of a meteor make a star. 30
O fix this fair Indefinite!
And 'mongst Thy shafts of sovereign light
Choose out that sure decisive dart
Which has the key of this close heart,
Knows all the corners of't, and can control
The self-shut cabinet of an unsearch'd soul.
O let it be at last Love's hour!
Raise this tall trophy of Thy power;
Come once the conquering way; not to confute
But kill this rebel-word, 'irresolute', 40
That so, in spite of all this peevish strength
Of weakness, she may write 'resolved at length'.
Unfold at length, unfold fair flower,
And use the season of Love's shower,
Meet His well-meaning wounds, wise heart!
And haste to drink the wholesome dart,

That healing shaft, which heav'n till now
Hath in Love's quiver hid for you.
O dart of Love! arrow of light!
O happy you, if it hit right!   50
It must not fall in vain, it must
Not mark the dry regardless dust.
Fair one, it is your fate; and brings
Eternal worlds upon its wings.
Meet it with wide-spread arms, and see
Its seat your soul's just centre be.
Disband dull fears, give faith the day;
To save your life, kill your delay.
It is Love's siege, and sure to be
Your triumph, though His victory.   60
'Tis cowardice that keeps this field,
And want of courage not to yield.
Yield then, O yield, that Love may win
The fort at last, and let life in.
Yield quickly, lest perhaps you prove
Death's prey, before the prize of Love.
This fort of your fair self, if 't be not won,
He is repulsed indeed, but you're undone.

From *Carmen Deo Nostro* (1652)

Charitas Nimia, or The Dear Bargain

Lord, what is man? why should he cost Thee
So dear? what had his ruin lost Thee?
Lord, what is man, that Thou hast over-bought
So much a thing of nought?

Love is too kind, I see; and can
Make but a simple merchant-man.
'Twas for such sorry merchandise
Bold painters have put out his eyes.

Alas, sweet Lord, what were't to Thee
If there were no such worms as we? 10
Heaven ne'ertheless still Heaven would be,
  Should mankind dwell
  In the deep Hell;
What have his woes to do with Thee?

  Let him go weep
  O'er his own wounds;
  Seraphim will not sleep,
Nor spheres let fall their faithful rounds.

Still would the youthful spirits sing;
And still Thy spacious palace ring; 20
Still would those beauteous ministers of light
  Burn all as bright,
And bow their flaming heads before Thee;
Still thrones and dominations would adore Thee;

Still would those ever wakeful sons of fire
  Keep warm Thy praise
  Both nights and days,
And teach Thy loved name to their noble lyre.

Let froward dust then do its kind,
And give itself for sport to the proud wind. 30
Why should a piece of peevish clay plead shares
In the eternity of Thy old cares?
Why should'st Thou bow Thy awful breast to see
What mine own madnesses have done with me?

Should not the king still keep his throne
Because some desperate fool's undone?
Or will the world's illustrious eyes
Weep for every worm that dies?
  Will the gallant sun
  E'er the less glorious run? 40

Will he hang down his golden head,
Or e'er the sooner seek his western bed,
      Because some foolish fly
      Grows wanton, and will die?

If I were lost in misery,
What was it to Thy Heav'n and Thee?
What was it to Thy precious blood,
If my foul heart called for a flood?

What if my faithless soul and I
      Would needs fall in   50
      With guilt and sin;
What did the Lamb that He should die?
What did the Lamb that He should need,
When the wolf sins, Himself to bleed?

      If my base lust
Bargained with Death and well-beseeming dust:
      Why should the white
      Lamb's bosom write
      The purple name
      Of my sin's shame?   60
Why should His unstained breast make good
My blushes with His Own heart-blood?

O my Saviour, make me see
How dearly Thou hast paid for me;
That lost again, my life may prove,
As then in death, so now in love.
           From *Carmen Deo Nostro* (1652)

An Epitaph upon a Young Married Couple, Dead and Buried Together

To these, whom Death again did wed,
This grave's their second marriage-bed;
For though the hand of Fate could force,
'Twixt soul and body, a divorce,
It could not sunder man and wife,
'Cause they both lived but one life.
Peace, good Reader, do not weep,
Peace, the lovers are asleep.
They, sweet turtles, folded lie
In the last knot Love could tie.   10
And though they lie as they were dead,
Their pillow stone, their sheets of lead:
(Pillow hard, and sheets not warm)
Love made the bed; they'll take no harm.
Let them sleep: let them sleep on,
Till this stormy night be gone,
Till the eternal morrow dawn;
Then the curtains will be drawn
And they wake into a light,
Whose Day shall never die in Night.   20

From *Carmen Deo Nostro* (1652)

RICHARD LOVELACE

Song. To Lucasta, Going beyond the Seas

If to be absent were to be
    Away from thee;
  Or that when I am gone
  You or I were alone;
Then, my Lucasta, might I crave
Pity from blustering wind, or swallowing wave.

But I'll not sigh one blast or gale
    To swell my sail,
  Or pay a tear to swage
  The foaming blue god's rage;   10
For whether he will let me pass
Or no, I'm still as happy as I was.

Though seas and land be 'twixt us both,
    Our faith and troth,
  Like separated souls,
  All time and space controls:
Above the highest sphere we meet
Unseen, unknown, and greet as angels greet.

So then we do anticipate
    Our after-fate,   20
  And are alive i' th' skies,
  If thus our lips and eyes
Can speak like spirits unconfin'd
In heaven, their earthy bodies left behind.

From Lucasta (1649)

Song. To Lucasta, Going to the Wars

Tell me not, sweet, I am unkind,
That from the nunnery
Of thy chaste breast and quiet mind,
To war and arms I fly.

True, a new mistress now I chase,
The first foe in the field;
And with a stronger faith embrace
A sword, a horse, a shield.

Yet this inconstancy is such
As you too shall adore;   10
I could not love thee, dear, so much,
Lov'd I not Honour more.

                              From *Lucasta* (1649)

Gratiana Dancing and Singing

See! with what constant motion,
Even and glorious as the sun,
  Gratiana steers that noble frame,
Soft as her breast, sweet as her voice
That gave each winding law and poise,
  And swifter than the wings of Fame.

She beat the happy pavement
By such a star made firmament,
  Which now no more the roof envies,
But swells up high with Atlas ev'n,   10
Bearing the brighter, nobler heav'n,
  And in her, all the deities.

Each step trod out a lover's thought
And the ambitious hopes he brought,
    Chained to her brave feet with such arts,
Such sweet command and gentle awe,
As when she ceased, we sighing saw
    The floor lay paved with broken hearts.

So did she move; so did she sing
Like the harmonious spheres that bring   20
    Unto their rounds their music's aid;
Which she performed such a way,
As all the enamoured world will say
    The Graces danced, and Apollo played.

                                From *Lucasta* (1649)

The Scrutiny

Why should you swear I am forsworn,
    Since thine I vowed to be?
Lady, it is already morn,
    And 'twas last night I swore to thee
That fond impossibility.

Have I not loved thee much and long,
    A tedious twelve hours' space?
I must all other beauties wrong,
    And rob thee of a new embrace,
Could I still dote upon thy face.   10

Not but all joy in thy brown hair
    By others may be found;
But I must search the black and fair,
    Like skilful mineralists that sound
For treasure in unploughed-up ground.

Then if, when I have loved my round,
   Thou prov'st the pleasant she,
With spoils of meaner beauties crowned,
   I laden will return to thee,
Ev'n sated with variety.   20

              From *Lucasta* (1649)

Princess Louisa Drawing

I saw a little deity,
Minerva in epitome,
Whom Venus, at first blush, surprised,
Took for her winged wag disguised;
But viewing then whereas she made
Not a distressed, but lively shade
Of Echo, whom he had betrayed,
Now wanton, and i' th' cool o' th' sun
With her delight a-hunting gone;
And thousands more, whom he had slain,   10
To live, and love, beloved again:
Ah, this is true divinity!
I will ungod that toy! cried she;
Then mark'd the Syrinx running fast
To Pan's embraces, with the haste
She fled him once, whose reed-pipe rent,
He finds now a new instrument.
Theseus returned, invokes the air
And winds, then wafts his fair;
Whilst Ariadne ravished stood   20
Half in his arms, half in the flood.

   Proud Anaxarete doth fall
At Iphis' feet, who smiles of all;
And he, whilst she his curls doth deck,
Hangs nowhere now, but on her neck.

                     K

Here Phoebus with a beam untombs
Long-hid Leucothoë, and dooms
Her father there; Daphne the fair
Knows now no bays but round her hair;
And to Apollo and his sons   30
Who pay him their due orisons,
Bequeaths her laurel-robe, that flame
Contemns, thunder and evil fame.

There kneeled Adonis fresh as spring,
Gay as his youth, now offering
Herself those joys with voice and hand,
Which first he could not understand.

Transfixed Venus stood amazed,
Full of the boy and love she gazed;
And in embraces seemed more   40
Senseless and cold than he before.
Useless child! In vain, said she,
You bear that fond artillery:
See here a power above the slow
Weak execution of thy bow.

So said, she rived the wood in two,
Unedged all his arrows too,
And with the string their feathers bound
To that part whence we have our wound.

See, see! the darts by which we burned   50
Are bright Louisa's pencils turned;
With which she now enliveth more
Beauties, than they destroyed before.

                         From *Lucasta* (1649)

The Grasshopper
To my noble friend, Mr. Charles Cotton. Ode

O thou that swing'st upon the waving hair
   Of some well-filled oaten beard,
Drunk every night with a delicious tear
   Dropt thee from heav'n, where now th'art reared;

The joys of earth and air are thine entire,
   That with thy feet and wings dost hop and fly;
And when thy poppy works thou dost retire
   To thy carved acorn-bed to lie.

Up with the day, the sun thou welcom'st then,
   Sport'st in the gilt-plats of his beams,   10
And all these merry days mak'st merry men,
   Thyself, and melancholy streams.

But ah the sickle! golden ears are cropt;
   Ceres and Bacchus bid good night;
Sharp frosty fingers all your flowers have topt,
   And what scythes spared, winds shave off quite.

Poor verdant fool, and now green ice! thy joys,
   Large and as lasting as thy perch of grass,
Bid us lay in 'gainst winter rain, and poise
   Their floods with an o'erflowing glass.   20

Thou best of men and friends! we will create
   A genuine Summer in each other's breast;
And spite of this cold Time and frozen Fate
   Thaw us a warm seat to our rest.

Our sacred hearths shall burn eternally
   As vestal flames; the North-wind, he
Shall strike his frost-stretch'd wings, dissolve and fly
   This Etna in epitome.

Dropping December shall come weeping in,
　　Bewail th'usurping of his reign;　　　　　　　　30
But when in showers of old Greek we begin,
　　Shall cry he hath his crown again.

Night as clear Hesper shall our tapers whip
　　From the light casements where we play,
And the dark hag from her black mantle strip,
　　And stick there everlasting day.

Thus richer than untempted kings are we,
　　That asking nothing, nothing need:
Though lord of all what seas embrace, yet he
　　That wants himself is poor indeed.　　　　　　40

　　　　　　　　　　　　From *Lucasta* (1649)

Song. To Althea, from Prison

When Love with unconfined wings
　　Hovers within my gates,
And my divine Althea brings
　　To whisper at the grates;
When I lie tangled in her hair,
　　And fetter'd to her eye,
The gods that wanton in the air
　　Know no such liberty.

When flowing cups run swiftly round
　　With no allaying Thames,　　　　　　　　　　10
Our careless heads with roses bound,
　　Our hearts with loyal flames;
When thirsty grief in wine we steep,
　　When healths and draughts go free,
Fishes that tipple in the deep
　　Know no such liberty.

When, like committed linnets, I
   With shriller throat shall sing
The sweetness, mercy, majesty,
   And glories of my king;   20
When I shall voice aloud how good
   He is, how great should be;
Enlarged winds that curl the flood
   Know no such liberty.

Stone walls do not a prison make,
   Nor iron bars a cage;
Minds innocent and quiet take
   That for an hermitage;
If I have freedom in my love,
   And in my soul am free,   30
Angels alone that soar above
   Enjoy such liberty.

                  From *Lucasta* (1649)

Love Enthroned. Ode

In truth, I do myself persuade
   That the wild boy is grown a man;
And all his childishness off laid,
   E'ere since Lucasta did his fires fan.
     He has left his apish jigs,
     And whipping hearts like gigs;
For t'other day I heard him swear
That Beauty should be crowned in Honour's chair.

With what a true and heavenly state
   He doth his glorious darts dispense,   10
Now cleansed from falsehood, blood, and hate,
   And newly tipped with innocence;
     Love Justice is become,

And doth the cruel doom:
Reversed is the old decree:
Behold! he sits enthroned with majesty.

Enthroned in Lucasta's eye,
  He doth our faith and hearts survey;
Then measures them by sympathy,
  And each to th'other's breast convey;   20
      Whilst to his altars now
      The frozen Vestals bow,
    And strict Diana, too, doth go
A-hunting with his feared, exchanged bow.

Th'embracing seas and ambient air
  Now in his holy fires burn;
Fish couple, birds and beasts in pair
  Do their own sacrifices turn.
      This is a miracle
      That might religion swell: 30
    But she, that these and their god awes,
Her crowned self submits to her own laws.
                    From *Lucasta, Posthume Poems* (1660)

HENRY VAUGHAN

To Amoret gone from him

Fancy and I, last evening, walked,
And Amoret, of thee we talked;
The west just then had stolen the sun,
And his last blushes were begun:
We sat, and marked how everything
Did mourn his absence; how the spring
That smiled and curled about his beams,
Whilst he was here, now checked her streams:
The wanton eddies of her face
Were taught less noise, and smoother grace;   10
And in a slow, sad channel went,
Whisp'ring the banks their discontent:
The careless ranks of flowers that spread
Their perfumed bosoms to his head,
And with an open, free embrace,
Did entertain his beamy face,
Like absent friends point to the west,
And on that weak reflection feast.
If creatures then that have no sense,
But the loose tie of influence,   20
Though fate and time each day remove
Those things that element their love,
At such vast distance can agree,
Why, Amoret, why should not we?

From *Poems* (1646)

The Retreat

Happy those early days, when I
Shined in my angel-infancy!

Before I understood this place
Appointed for my second race,
Or taught my soul to fancy ought
But a white, celestial thought;
When yet I had not walked above
A mile or two from my first love,
And looking back (at that short space),
Could see a glimpse of His bright face: 10
When on some gilded cloud, or flower,
My gazing soul would dwell an hour,
And in those weaker glories spy
Some shadows of eternity;
Before I taught my tongue to wound
My conscience with a sinful sound,
Or had the black art to dispense
A sev'ral sin to ev'ry sense,
But felt through all this fleshly dress
Bright shoots of everlastingness.   20

O how I long to travel back
And tread again that ancient track!
That I might once more reach that plain,
Where first I left my glorious train;
From whence th'enlighten'd spirit sees
That shady city of palm trees.
But ah! my soul with too much stay
Is drunk, and staggers in the way.
Some men a forward motion love,
But I by backward steps would move;   30
And when this dust falls to the urn,
In that state I came, return.

                    From *Silex Scintillans* (1650)

The Morning-watch

O joys! infinite sweetness! with what flowers
And shoots of glory my soul breaks and buds!
       All the long hours
       Of night and rest,
       Through the still shrouds
       Of sleep and clouds,
       This dew fell on my breast;
       O how it bloods,
And spirits all my earth! hark! in what rings
And hymning circulations the quick world   10
       Awakes, and sings!
       The rising winds,
       And falling springs,
       Birds, beasts, all things
       Adore Him in their kinds.
       Thus all is hurl'd
In sacred hymns and order, the great chime
And symphony of Nature. Prayer is
       The world in tune,
       A spirit-voice,   20
       And vocal joys,
       Whose echo is heaven's bliss.
       O let me climb
When I lie down! The pious soul by night
Is like a clouded star, whose beams, though said
       To shed their light
       Under some cloud,
       Yet are above,
       And shine and move   30
       Beyond that misty shroud.
       So in my bed,
That curtained grave, though sleep, like ashes, hide
My lamp and life, both shall in Thee abide.

From *Silex Scintillans* (1650)

Corruption

Sure, it was so. Man in those early days
    Was not all stone and earth;
He shined a little, and by those weak rays
    Had some glimpse of his birth.
He saw heaven o'er his head, and knew from whence
    He came, condemned, hither;
And, as first love draws strongest, so from hence
    His mind sure progressed thither.
Things here were strange unto him; sweat and till;
    All was a thorn or weed;   10
Nor did those last, but (like himself) died still
    As soon as they did seed;
They seemed to quarrel with him; for that act,
    That fell him, foiled them all;
He drew the curse upon the world, and crack'd
    The whole frame with his fall.
This made him long for home, as loth to stay
    With murmurers and foes;
He sighed for Eden, and would often say
    'Ah! what bright days were those!'   20
Nor was heav'n cold unto him; for each day
    The valley or the mountain
Afforded visits, and still Paradise lay
    In some green shade or fountain.
Angels lay leiger here; each bush and cell,
    Each oak and highway knew them;
Walk but the fields, or sit down at some well,
    And he was sure to view them.
Almighty Love! where art Thou now? mad man
    Sits down and freezeth on;   30
He raves, and swears to stir nor fire, nor fan,
    But bids the thread be spun.
I see, Thy curtains are close-drawn; Thy bow
    Looks dim too in the cloud;

Sin triumphs still, and man is sunk below
    The centre, and his shroud.
All's in deep sleep and night: thick darkness lies
    And hatcheth o'er Thy people;
But hark! what trumpet's that? what angel cries
      'Arise! thrust in Thy sickle.'?   40
        From *Silex Scintillans* (1650)

Affliction

Peace, peace; it is not so. Thou dost miscall
    Thy physic: pills that change
Thy sick accessions into settled health;
This is the great elixir, that turns gall
To wine and sweetness, poverty to wealth,
    And brings man home when he doth range.
    Did not He, who ordained the day,
        Ordain night too?
    And in the greater world display
    What in the lesser He would do?   10
All flesh is clay, thou knowest; and but that God
    Doth use His rod,
And by a fruitful change of frosts and showers
    Cherish, and bind thy powers,
Thou wouldst to weeds and thistles quite disperse,
    And be more wild than is thy verse.
Sickness is wholesome, and crosses are but curbs
    To check the mule, unruly man;
They are heaven's husbandry, the famous fan,
    Purging the floor which chaff disturbs.   20
Were all the year one constant sunshine, we
    Should have no flowers;
All would be drought and leanness; not a tree
    Would make us bowers.

Beauty consists in colours; and that's best
    Which is not fixed, but flies and flows;
The settled red is dull, and whites that rest
    Something of sickness would disclose.
       Vicissitude plays all the game;
          Nothing that stirs,   30
          Or hath a name,
       But waits upon this wheel;
Kingdoms too have their physic, and for steel
    Exchange their peace and furs.
Thus doth God key disordered man,
       Which none else can,
    Tuning his breast to rise or fall;
And by a sacred, needful art
Like strings stretch ev'ry part,
    Making the whole most musical.   40
        From *Silex Scintillans* (1650)

The World

I saw Eternity the other night,
Like a great ring of pure and endless light,
    All calm, as it was bright;
And round beneath it, Time in hours, days, years,
       Driv'n by the spheres
Like a vast shadow mov'd; in which the world
    And all her train were hurled.
The doting lover in his quaintest strain
       Did there complain;
Near him, his lute, his fancy, and his flights,   10
       Wit's sour delights;
With gloves, and knots, the silly snares of pleasure,
       Yet his dear treasure,
All scattered lay, while he his eyes did pour
       Upon a flow'r.

The darksome statesman, hung with weights and woe,
Like a thick midnight-fog, moved there so slow,
   He did not stay, nor go;
Condemning thoughts (like sad eclipses) scowl
     Upon his soul,   20
And clouds of crying witnesses without
   Pursued him with one shout.
Yet digg'd the mole, and lest his ways be found,
    Worked underground,
Where he did clutch his prey; but one did see
    That policy:
Churches and altars fed him; perjuries
    Were gnats and flies;
It rained about him blood and tears, but he
    Drank them as free.   30

The fearful miser on a heap of rust
Sat pining all his life there, did scarce trust
   His own hands with the dust,
Yet would not place one piece above, but lives
    In fear of thieves.
Thousands there were as frantic as himself,
   And hugged each one his pelf;
The downright epicure placed heav'n in sense,
    And scorned pretence;
While others, slipp'd into a wide excess,   40
    Said little less;
The weaker sort slight, trivial wares enslave,
    Who think them brave;
And poor, despised Truth sat counting by
    Their victory.

Yet some who all this while did weep and sing,
And sing and weep, soared up into the ring;
   But most would use no wing.
'O fools,' said I, 'thus to prefer dark night
    Before true light!   50

To live in grots and caves, and hate the day
    Because it shows the way;
The way which from this dead and dark abode
    Leads up to God;
A way where you might tread the sun, and be
    More bright than he.'
But as I did their madness so discuss,
    One whispered thus,
'This ring the Bridegroom did for none provide,
    But for His bride.'   60

          From *Silex Scintillans* (1650)

Man

    Weighing the steadfastness and state
Of some mean things which here below reside,
Where birds, like watchful clocks, the noiseless date
    And intercourse of times divide,
Where bees at night get home and hive, and flow'rs,
    Early as well as late,
Rise with the sun and set in the same bow'rs;

    I would, said I, my God would give
The staidness of these things to man! for these
To His divine appointments ever cleave,   10
    And no new business breaks their peace;
The birds nor sow nor reap, yet sup and dine;
    The flow'rs without clothes live,
Yet Solomon was never dressed so fine.

    Man hath still either toys, or care;
He hath no root, nor to one place is tied,
But ever restless and irregular
    About this earth doth run and ride.

He knows he hath a home, but scarce knows where;
    He says it is so far,   20
That he hath quite forgot how to go there.

    He knocks at all doors, strays and roams,
Nay, hath not so much wit as some stones have,
Which in the darkest nights point to their homes,
    By some hid sense their Maker gave;
Man is the shuttle, to whose winding quest
        And passage through these looms
God ordered motion, but ordained no rest.

           From *Silex Scintillans* (1650)

Cock-crowing

    Father of lights! what sunny seed,
    What glance of day hast Thou confined
    Into this bird? To all the breed
    This busy ray Thou hast assigned;
        Their magnetism works all night,
        And dreams of Paradise and light.

    Their eyes watch for the morning hue,
    Their little grain, expelling night,
    So shines and sings, as if it knew
    The path unto the house of light.   10
        It seems their candle, howe'er done,
        Was tinned and lighted at the sun.

    If such a tincture, such a touch,
    So firm a longing can empower,
    Shall Thy own image think it much
    To watch for Thy appearing hour?
        If a mere blast so fill the sail,
        Shall not the breath of God prevail?

O Thou immortal light and heat!
Whose hand so shines through all this frame,   20
That by the beauty of the seat,
We plainly see Who made the same;
    Seeing Thy seed abides in me,
    Dwell Thou in it, and I in Thee!

To sleep without Thee is to die;
Yea, 'tis a death partakes of hell;
For where Thou dost not close the eye
It never opens, I can tell.
    In such a dark, Egyptian border,
    The shades of death dwell, and disorder.   30

If joys and hopes and earnest throes
And hearts, whose pulse beats still for light,
Are given to birds; who, but Thee, knows
A love-sick soul's exalted flight?
    Can souls be track'd by any eye
    But His, who gave them wings to fly?

Only this veil which Thou hast broke,
And must be broken yet in me,
This veil, I say, is all the cloak
And cloud which shadows Thee from me.   40
    This veil Thy full-eyed love denies,
    And only gleams and fractions spies.

O take it off! make no delay;
But brush me with Thy light, that I
May shine unto a perfect day,
And warm me at Thy glorious eye!
    O take it off! or till it flee,
    Though with no lily, stay with me!
                From *Silex Scintillans* (1650)

The Bird

Hither thou com'st: the busy wind all night
Blew through thy lodging, where thy own warm wing
Thy pillow was. Many a sullen storm,
For which coarse man seems much the fitter born,
      Rain'd on thy bed
      And harmless head.

And now as fresh and cheerful as the light
Thy little heart in early hymns doth sing
Unto that Providence, whose unseen arm
Curb'd them, and cloth'd thee well and warm.   10
    All things that be praise Him; and had
    Their lesson taught them when first made.

So hills and valleys into singing break;
And though poor stones have neither speech nor tongue,
While active winds and streams both run and speak,
Yet stones are deep in admiration.
Thus praise and prayer here beneath the sun
Make lesser mornings, when the great are done.

For each enclosed spirit is a star
    Enlight'ning his own little sphere,   20
Whose light, though fetched and borrowed from far,
    Both mornings makes and evenings there.

But as these birds of light make a land glad,
Chirping their solemn matins on each tree:
So in the shades of night some dark fowls be,
Whose heavy notes make all that hear them sad.

    The turtle then in palm trees mourns,
      While owls and satyrs howl;
    The pleasant land to brimstone turns,
      And all her streams grow foul.   30

Brightness and mirth, and love and faith, all fly,
Till the day-spring breaks forth again from high.

From Silex Scintillans (1650)

The Timber

Sure thou didst flourish once! and many springs,
Many bright mornings, much dew, many showers
Passed o'er thy head; many light hearts and wings,
Which now are dead, lodg'd in thy living bowers.

And still a new succession sings and flies;
Fresh groves grow up, and their green branches shoot
Towards the old and still enduring skies,
While the low violet thrives at their root.

But thou beneath the sad and heavy line
Of death dost waste all senseless, cold, and dark;   10
Where not so much as dreams of light may shine,
Nor any thought of greenness, leaf or bark.

And yet, (as if some deep hate and dissent,
Bred in thy growth betwixt high winds and thee,
Were still alive), thou dost great storms resent
Before they come, and knowest how near they be.

Else all at rest thou liest, and the fierce breath
Of tempests can no more disturb thy ease;
But this thy strange resentment after death
Means only those who broke (in life) thy peace.   20

So murthered man, when lovely life is done,
And his blood freez'd, keeps in the centre still
Some secret sense, which makes the dead blood run
At his approach that did the body kill.

And is there any murth'rer worse than sin?
Or any storms more foul than a lewd life?
Or what resentient can work more within,
Than true remorse, when with past sins at strife?

He that hath left life's vain joys and vain care,
And truly hates to be detain'd on earth,   30
Hath got an house where many mansions are,
And keeps his soul unto eternal mirth.

But though thus dead unto the world, and ceased
From sin, he walks a narrow, private way;
Yet grief and old wounds make him sore displeased
And all his life a rainy, weeping day.

For though he should forsake the world, and live
As mere a stranger, as men long since dead;
Yet joy itself will make a right soul grieve
To think he should be so long vainly led.   40

But as shades set off light, so tears and grief
(Though of themselves but a sad blubbered story)
By showing the sin great, show the relief
Far greater, and so speak my Saviour's glory.

If my way lies through deserts and wild woods,
Where all the land with scorching heat is curst;
Better the pools should flow with rain and floods
To fill my bottle, than I die with thirst.

Blest showers they are, and streams sent from above
Begetting virgins where they use to flow;   50
And trees of life no other waters love;
These upper springs, and none else make them grow.

But these chaste fountains flow not till we die:
Some drops may fall before, but a clear spring

And ever running, till we leave to fling
Dirt in her way, will keep above the sky.

From *Silex Scintillans* (1650)

The Rainbow

Still young and fine! but what is still in view
We slight as old and soiled, though fresh and new.
How bright wert thou, when Shem's admiring eye
Thy burnished, flaming arch did first descry!
When Terah, Nahor, Haran, Abram, Lot,
The youthful world's grey fathers in one knot,
Did with intentive looks watch every hour
For thy new light, and trembled at each shower!
When thou dost shine, darkness looks white and fair,
Storms turn to music, clouds to smiles and air: 10
Rain gently spends his honey-drops, and pours
Balm on the cleft earth, milk on grass and flowers.
Bright pledge of peace and sunshine! the sure tie
Of thy Lord's hand, the object of His eye.
When I behold thee, though my light be dim,
Distant and low, I can in thine see Him,
Who looks upon thee from His glorious throne,
And minds the covenant 'twixt All and One.
O foul, deceitful men! my God doth keep
His promise still, but we break ours and sleep.   20
After the Fall, the first sin was in blood,
And drunkenness quickly did succeed the flood;
But since Christ died (as if we did devise
To lose Him too, as well as Paradise),
These two grand sins we join and act together,
Though blood and drunkenness make but foul, foul weather.
Water (though both heaven's windows and the deep
Full forty days o'er the drowned world did weep),
Could not reform us; and blood, in despite,

Yea, God's own blood, we tread upon and slight.   30
So those bad daughters, which God saved from fire,
While Sodom yet did smoke, lay with their sire.

Then peaceful, signal bow, but in a cloud
Still lodged, where all thy unseen arrows shroud,
I will on thee as on a comet look,
A comet, the sad world's ill-boding book;
Thy light as luctual and stained with woes
I'll judge, where penal flames sit mixed and close;
For though some think thou shinest but to restrain
Bold storms, and simply dost attend on rain;   40
Yet I know well, and so our sins require,
Thou dost but court cold rain, till rain turns fire.

                              From *Silex Scintillans* (1650)

Childhood

I cannot reach it; and my striving eye
Dazzles at it, as at eternity.

Were now that chronicle alive,
Those white designs which children drive,
And the thoughts of each harmless hour,
With their content too in my power,
Quickly would I make my path even,
And by mere playing go to heaven.

Why should men love
A wolf, more than a lamb or dove?   10
Or choose hell-fire and brimstone streams
Before bright stars and God's own beams?
Who kisseth thorns will hurt his face,
But flowers do both refresh and grace;
And sweetly living (fie on men!)

Are, when dead, medicinal then;
If seeing much should make staid eyes,
And long experience should make wise;
Since all that age doth teach is ill,
Why should I not love childhood still?   20
Why, if I see a rock or shelf,
Shall I from thence cast down myself?
Or by complying with the world,
From the same precipice be hurled?
Those observations are but foul,
Which make me wise to lose my soul.

And yet the practice worldings call
Business, and weighty action all,
Checking the poor child for his play,
But gravely cast themselves away.   30

  Dear, harmless age! the short, swift span
Where weeping virtue parts with man;
Where love without lust dwells, and bends
What way we please, without self-ends.

An age of mysteries! which he
Must live twice, that would God's face see;
Which angels guard, and with it play,
Angels! which foul men drive away.

How do I study now, and scan
Thee more than e'er I studied man,   40
And only see through a long night
Thy edges and thy bordering light!
O for thy centre and mid-day!
For sure that is the narrow way!

From *Silex Scintillans* (1650)

The Waterfall

With what deep murmurs, through Time's silent stealth,
Doth thy transparent, cool, and wat'ry wealth,
      Here flowing fall,
      And chide and call,
As if his liquid, loose retinue stay'd
Ling'ring, and were of this steep place afraid,
      The common pass,
      Where clear as glass,
      All must descend
      Not to an end,   10
But quickened by this deep and rocky grave,
Rise to a longer course more bright and brave.

    Dear stream! dear bank! where often I
    Have sat, and pleased my pensive eye,
    Why, since each drop of thy quick store
    Runs thither whence it flowed before,
    Should poor souls fear a shade or night,
    Who came, sure, from a sea of light?
    Or, since those drops are all sent back
    So sure to Thee that none doth lack,   20
    Why should frail flesh doubt any more
    That what God takes He'll not restore?
    O useful element and clear!
    My sacred wash and cleanser here;
    My first consigner unto those
    Fountains of life, where the Lamb goes!
    What sublime truths and wholesome themes
    Lodge in thy mystical, deep streams!
    Such as dull man can never find,
    Unless that Spirit lead his mind,   30
    Which first upon thy face did move,
    And hatched all with His quick'ning love.
    As this loud brook's incessant fall
    In streaming rings restagnates all,

Which reach by course the bank, and then
Are no more seen: just so pass men.
O my invisible estate,
My glorious liberty, still late!
Thou art the channel my soul seeks,
Not this with cataracts and creeks.   40

From *Silex Scintillans* (1650)

'They are all gone into the world of light'

They are all gone into the world of light!
    And I alone sit ling'ring here;
Their very memory is fair and bright,
    And my sad thoughts doth clear.

It glows and glitters in my cloudy breast,
    Like stars upon some gloomy grove,
Or those faint beams in which this hill is dressed,
    After the sun's remove.

I see them walking in an air of glory,
    Whose light doth trample on my days: 10
My days, which are at best but dull and hoary,
    Mere glimmering and decays.

O holy Hope! and high Humility,
    High as the heavens above!
These are your walks, and you have showed them me,
    To kindle my cold love.

Dear, beauteous Death! the jewel of the just,
    Shining nowhere, but in the dark;
What mysteries do lie beyond thy dust,
    Could man outlook that mark!   20

He that hath found some fledged bird's nest, may know
    At first sight if the bird be flown;
But what fair well or grove he sings in now,
    That is to him unknown.

And yet, as angels in some brighter dreams
    Call to the soul when man doth sleep,
So some strange thoughts transcend our wonted themes,
    And into glory peep.

If a star were confin'd into a tomb,
    Her captive flames must needs burn there;   30
But when the hand that locked her up, gives room,
    She'll shine through all the sphere.

O Father of eternal life, and all
    Created glories under Thee!
Resume Thy spirit from this world of thrall
    Into true liberty.

Either disperse these mists, which blot and fill
    My perspective, still, as they pass:
Or else remove me hence unto that hill
    Where I shall need no glass.   40
                From *Silex Scintillans* (1650)

ANDREW MARVELL

The Nymph Complaining for the Death of her Faun

The wanton troopers riding by
Have shot my Faun, and it will die.
Ungentle men! They cannot thrive
To kill thee. Thou ne'er didst alive
Them any harm: alas, nor could
Thy death yet do them any good.
I'm sure I never wished them ill:
Nor do I for all this, nor will;
But if my simple prayers may yet
Prevail with Heav'n to forget   10
Thy murder, I will join my tears
Rather than fail. But, O my fears!
It cannot die so, Heaven's King
Keeps register of everything,
And nothing may we use in vain.
Ev'n beasts must be with justice slain;
Else men are made their Deodands.
Though they should wash their guilty hands
In this warm life blood, which doth part
From thine, and wound me to the heart,   20
Yet could they not be clean: their stain
Is dyed in such a purple grain.
There is not such another in
The world, to offer for their sin.
   Unconstant Sylvio, when yet
I had not found him counterfeit,
One morning (I remember well)
Tied in this silver chain and bell,
Gave it to me: nay, and I know
What he said then: I'm sure I do.   30
Said he, 'Look how your huntsmen here
Hath taught a faun to hunt his Dear.'

But Sylvio soon had me beguiled.
This waxed tame, while he grew wild,
And quite regardless of my smart
Left me his Faun, but took his heart.

   Thenceforth I set myself to play
My solitary time away,
With this: and very well content
Could so mine idle life have spent.   40
For it was full of sport, and light
Of foot, and heart: and did invite
Me to its game: it seemed to bless
Itself in me. How could I less
Than love it? O I cannot be
Unkind, to a beast that loveth me.

   Had it liv'd long, I do not know
Whether it too might have done so
As Sylvio did: his gifts might be
Perhaps as false or more than he.   50
But I am sure, for aught that I
Could in so short a time espy,
Thy love was far more better then
The love of false and cruel men.

   With sweetest milk, and sugar, first
I it at mine own fingers nursed.
And as it grew, so every day
It waxed more white and sweet than they.
It had so sweet a breath! And oft
I blush'd to see its foot more soft   60
And white (shall I say then my hand?),
Nay, any lady's in the land.

   It is a wondrous thing, how fleet
'Twas on those little silver feet.
With what a pretty skipping grace
It oft would challenge me the race:
And when 'thad left me far away,
'Twould stay, and run again, and stay.
For it was nimbler much than hinds,

And trod, as on the four winds.   70
   I have a garden of my own,
But so with roses overgrown,
And lilies that you would it guess
To be a little wilderness.
And all the spring time of the year
It only loved to be there.
Among the beds of lilies I
Have sought it oft, where it should lie,
Yet could not, till itself would rise,
Find it, although before mine eyes.   80
For, in the flaxen lilies' shade,
It like a bank of lilies laid.
Upon the roses it would feed,
Until its lips ev'n seemed to bleed:
And then to me 'twould boldly trip,
And print those roses on my lip.
But all its chief delight was still
On roses thus itself to fill:
And its pure virgin limbs to fold
In whitest sheets of lilies cold.   90
Had it liv'd long, it would have been
Lilies without, roses within.
   O help! O help! I see it faint,
And die as calmly as a saint.
See how it weeps. The tears do come
Sad, slowly dropping like a gum.
So weeps the wounded balsam, so
The holy frankincense doth flow.
The brotherless Heliades
Melt in such amber tears as these.   100
   I in a golden vial will
Keep these two crystal tears: and fill
It till it do o'erflow with mine,
Then place it in Diana's shrine.
   Now my sweet Faun is vanish'd to
Whither the swans and turtles go:

In fair Elysium to endure
With milk-white lambs, and ermins pure.
O do not run too fast: for I
Will but bespeak thy grave, and die.   110
    First my unhappy statue shall
Be cut in marble; and withal,
Let it be weeping too: but there
The engraver sure his art may spare;
For I so truly thee bemoan,
That I shall weep, though I be stone:
Until my tears, still dropping, wear
My breast, themselves engraving there.
There at my feet shalt thou be laid,
Of purest alabaster made: 120
For I would have thine image be
White as I can, though not as thee.

                    From *Miscellaneous Poems* (1681)

Bermudas

Where the remote Bermudas ride
In the Ocean's bosom unespied,
From a small boat, that rowed along,
The list'ning winds received this Song.
    'What should we do but sing His praise
That led us through the wat'ry maze,
Unto an Isle so long unknown,
And yet far kinder than our own?
Where He the huge sea-monsters wracks,
That lift the deep upon their backs.   10
He lands us on a grassy stage,
Safe from the storms and Prelate's rage.
He gave us this eternal spring,
Which here enamels everything:
And sends the fowls to us in care

On daily visits through the air.
He hangs in shades the orange bright,
Like golden lamps in a green night,
And does in the pomegranates close
Jewels more rich than Ormus shows.   20
He makes the figs our mouths to meet,
And throws the melons at our feet,
But apples plants of such a price
No tree could ever bear them twice.
With cedars, chosen by His hand,
From Lebanon, he stores the land,
And makes the hollow seas, that roar,
Proclaim the ambergris on shore.
He cast (of which we rather boast)
The Gospel's pearl upon our coast,   30
And in these rocks for us did frame
A temple, where to sound His name.
O let our voice His praise exalt,
Till it arrive at Heaven's vault:
Which thence (perhaps) rebounding, may
Echo beyond the Mexique Bay.'
Thus sang they, in the English boat,
An holy and a cheerful note,
And all the way, to guide their chime,
With falling oars they kept the time.   40

From *Miscellaneous Poems* (1681)

To his Coy Mistress

Had we but World enough, and Time,
This coyness, Lady, were no crime.
We would sit down, and think which way
To walk, and pass our long love's day.
Thou by the Indian Ganges' side
Shouldst rubies find: I by the tide

Of Humber would complain. I would
Love you ten years before the Flood:
And you should, if you please, refuse
Till the conversion of the Jews.   10
My vegetable love should grow
Vaster than empires, and more slow.
An hundred years should go to praise
Thine eyes, and on thy forehead gaze;
Two hundred to adore each breast:
But thirty thousand to the rest.
An age at least to every part,
And the last age should show your heart;
For, Lady, you deserve this state,
Nor would I love at lower rate.   20
    But at my back I always hear
Time's winged chariot hurrying near:
And yonder all before us lie
Deserts of vast Eternity.
Thy beauty shall no more be found,
Nor, in thy marble vault, shall sound
My echoing song: then worms shall try
That long preserv'd virginity:
And your quaint honour turn to dust,
And into ashes all my lust.   30
The grave's a fine and private place,
But none, I think, do there embrace.
    Now therefore, while the youthful hue
Sits on thy skin like morning dew,
And while thy willing soul transpires
At every pore with instant fires,
Now let us sport us while we may;
And now, like am'rous birds of prey,
Rather at once our time devour,
Than languish in his slow-chapt pow'r.   40
Let us roll all our strength and all
Our sweetness up into one ball,
And tear our pleasures with rough strife

Thorough the iron gates of life.
Thus, though we cannot make our sun
Stand still, yet we will make him run.

From *Miscellaneous Poems* (1681)

Damon the Mower

Hark how the mower Damon sung,
With love of Juliana stung!
While ev'rything did seem to paint
The scene more fit for his complaint.
Like her fair eyes the day was fair,
But scorching like his am'rous care.
Sharp, like his scythe, his sorrow was,
And wither'd like his hopes the grass.

'O what unusual heats are here,
Which thus our sun-burned meadows sear!   10
The grasshopper its pipe gives o'er,
And hamstring'd frogs can dance no more.
But in the brook the green frog wades,
And grasshoppers seek out the shades.
Only the snake, that kept within,
Now glitters in its second skin.

'This heat the sun could never raise,
Nor dog-star so inflames the days.
It from an higher beauty grow'th,
Which burns the fields and mower both: 20
Which made the dog, and makes the sun
Hotter than his own Phaeton.
Not July causeth these extremes,
But Juliana's scorching beams.

'Tell me where I may pass the fires
Of the hot day, or hot desires.
To what cool cave shall I descend,
Or to what gelid fountain bend?
Alas! I look for ease in vain,
When remedies themselves complain.   30
No moisture but my tears to rest,
Nor cold but in her icy breast.

'How long wilt thou, fair shepherdess,
Esteem me, and my presents less?
To thee the harmless snake I bring,
Disarmed of its teeth and sting.
To thee chameleons changing hue,
And oak leaves tipp'd with honey dew.
Yet thou, ungrateful, hast not sought
Nor what they are, nor who them brought.   40

'I am the Mower Damon, known
Through all the meadows I have mown.
On me the morn her dew distils
Before her darling daffodils.
And if at noon my toil me heat,
The sun himself licks off my sweat:
While, going home, the ev'ning sweet
In cowslip water bathes my feet.

'What, though the piping shepherd stock
The plains with an unnumbered stock,   50
This scythe of mine discovers wide
More ground than all his sheep do hide.
With this the golden fleece I shear
Of all these closes ev'ry year;
And, though in wool more poor than they,
Yet am I richer far in hay.

'Nor am I so deformed to sight
If in my scythe I looked right,

In which I see my picture done,
As in a crescent moon the sun.   60
The deathless fairies take me oft
To lead them in their dances soft:
And, when I tune myself to sing,
About me they contract their ring.

'How happy might I still have mow'd,
Had not Love here his thistles sow'd!
But now I all the day complain,
Joining my labour to my pain;
And with my scythe cut down the grass,
Yet still my grief is where it was: 70
But, when the iron blunter grows,
Sighing I whet my scythe and woes.'

While thus he threw his elbow round,
Depopulating all the ground,
And, with his whistling scythe, does cut
Each stroke between the earth and root,
The edged steel by careless chance
Did into his own ankle glance;
And there among the grass fell down,
By his own scythe, the mower mown.   80

'Alas!' said he, 'these hurts are slight
To those that die by love's despite.
With shepherd's-purse, and clown's-all-heal,
The blood I staunch, and wound I seal.
Only for him no cure is found,
Whom Juliana's eyes do wound,
'Tis death alone that this must do;
For death, thou art a mower too.'

From *Miscellaneous Poems* (1681)

The Mower to the Glow-worms

Ye living lamps, by whose dear light
The nightingale does sit so late,
And studying all the summer-night,
Her matchless songs does meditate;

Ye country comets, that portend
No war, nor prince's funeral,
Shining unto no higher end
Than to presage the grasses' fall;

Ye glow-worms, whose officious flame
To wand'ring mowers shows the way,   10
That in the night have lost their aim,
And after foolish fires do stray;

Your courteous lights in vain you waste,
Since Juliana here is come,
For she my mind hath so displaced
That I shall never find my home.

From *Miscellaneous Poems* (1681)

The Gallery

Clora, come view my soul, and tell
Whether I have contrived it well.
Now all its several lodgings lie
Composed into one Gallery;
And the great arras-hangings, made
Of various faces, by are laid;
That, for all furniture, you'll find
Only your picture in my mind.

Here thou art painted in the dress

Of an inhuman murderess;   10
Examining upon our hearts
Thy fertile shop of cruel arts;
Engines more keen than ever yet
Adorned tyrant's cabinet;
Of which the most tormenting are
Black eyes, red lips, and curled hair.

But, on the other side, th'art drawn
Like to Aurora in the dawn;
When in the east she slumb'ring lies,
And stretches out her milky thighs;   20
While all the morning quire does sing,
And manna falls, and roses spring:
And, at thy feet, the wooing doves
Sit perfecting their harmless loves.

Like an enchantress here thou show'st,
Vexing thy restless Lover's ghost;
And, by a light obscure, dost rave
Over his entrails, in the cave;
Divining thence, with horrid care,
How long thou shalt continue fair;   30
And (when informed) them throw'st away,
To be the greedy vulture's prey.

But, against that, thou sit'st afloat
Like Venus in her pearly boat.
The Halcyons, calming all that's nigh,
Betwixt the air and water fly.
Or, if some rolling wave appears,
A mass of ambergris it bears.
Nor blows more wind than what may well
Convoy the perfume to the smell.   40

These pictures and a thousand more,
Of thee, my Gallery do store;

In all the forms thou canst invent
Either to please me, or torment:
For thou alone to people me
Art grown a num'rous colony;
And a Collection choicer far
Than or Whitehall's, or Mantua's were.

But, of these pictures and the rest,
That at the entrance likes me best: 50
Where the same posture, and the look
Remains, with which I first was took.
A tender Shepherdess, whose hair
Hangs loosely playing in the air,
Transplanting flow'rs from the green hill,
To crown her head, and bosom fill.

From *Miscellaneous Poems* (1681)

The Garden

How vainly men themselves amaze
To win the palm, the oak, or bays;
And their uncessant labours see
Crowned from some single herb or tree,
Whose short and narrow verged shade
Does prudently their toils upraid;
While all flow'rs and all trees do close
To weave the garlands of repose.

Fair Quiet, have I found thee here,
And Innocence, thy sister dear?   10
Mistaken long, I sought you then
In busy companies of men.
Your sacred plants, if here below,
Only among the plants will grow.
Society is all but rude
To this delicious solitude.

No white nor red was ever seen
So am'rous as this lovely green.
Fond lovers, cruel as their flame,
Cut in these trees their mistress' name.   20
Little, alas, they know, or heed,
How far these beauties hers exceed!
Fair trees! where s'eer your barks I wound,
No name shall but your own be found.

When we have run our passions' heat,
Love hither makes his best retreat.
The gods, that mortal beauty chase,
Still in a tree did end their race.
Apollo hunted Daphne so,
Only that she might laurel grow.   30
And Pan did after Syrinx speed
Not as a nymph, but for a reed.

What wond'rous life in this I lead!
Ripe apples drop about my head;
The luscious clusters of the vine
Upon my mouth do crush their wine;
The nectarine, and curious peach
Into my hands themselves do reach;
Stumbling on melons, as I pass,
Ensnared with flow'rs, I fall on grass.   40

Meanwhile the mind from pleasure less
Withdraws into its happiness:
The mind, that Ocean where each kind
Does straight its own resemblance find;
Yet it creates, transcending these,
Far other worlds, and other seas;
Annihilating all that's made
To a green thought in a green shade.

Here at the fountain's sliding foot,

Or at some fruit-tree's mossy root,   50
Casting the body's vest aside,
My soul into the boughs does glide;
There, like a bird, it sits and sings,
Then whets, and combs its silver wings,
And, till prepared for longer flight,
Waves in its plumes the various light.

Such was that happy Garden-state
While man there walked without a mate;
After a place so pure, and sweet,
What other help could yet be meet!   60
But 'twas beyond a mortal's share
To wander solitary there:
Two Paradises 'twere in one
To live in Paradise alone.

How well the skilful Gard'ner drew
Of flow'rs and herbs this dial new;
Where, from above, the milder sun
Does from a fragrant Zodiac run;
And, as it works, th'industrious bee
Computes its time as well as we.   70
How could such sweet and wholesome hours
Be reckoned, but with herbs and flow'rs!
                    From *Miscellaneous Poems* (1681)

An Horatian Ode Upon Cromwell's Return from Ireland

The forward youth that would appear
Must now forsake his Muses dear,
    Nor in the shadows sing
    His numbers languishing.

'Tis time to leave the books in dust,
And oil the unused armour's rust,

Removing from the wall
The corslet of the hall.

So restless Cromwell could not cease
In the inglorious arts of peace,   10
    But through adventurous war
    Urged his active star:

And, like the three-fork'd lightning, first
Breaking the clouds where it was nursed,
    Did thorough his own side
    His fiery way divide.

For 'tis all one to courage high,
The emulous, or enemy;
    And with such, to enclose
    Is more than to oppose.   20

Then burning through the air he went,
And palaces and temples rent:
    And Caesar's head at last
    Did through his laurels blast.

'Tis madness to resist or blame
The force of angry Heaven's flame;
    And, if we would speak true,
    Much to the man is due,

Who, from his private gardens, where
He lived reserved and austere,   30
    As if his highest plot
    To plant the bergamot,

Could by industrious valour climb
To ruin the great work of time,
    And cast the Kingdom old
    Into another mould.

Though Justice against Fate complain,
And plead the ancient rights in vain:
  But those do hold or break
  As men are strong or weak: 40

Nature, that hateth emptiness,
Allows of penetration less,
  And therefore must make room
  Where greater spirits come.

What field of all the Civil Wars,
Where his were not the deepest scars?
  And Hampton shows what part
  He had of wiser art:

Where, twining subtle fears with hope,
He wove a net of such a scope   50
  That Charles himself might chase
  To Carisbrook's narrow case:

That thence the Royal Actor borne
The tragic scaffold might adorn;
  While round the armed bands
  Did clap their bloody hands.

He nothing common did or mean
Upon that memorable scene,
  But with his keener eye
  The axe's edge did try: 60

Nor called the Gods, with vulgar spite,
To vindicate his helpless Right,
  But bowed his comely head
  Down, as upon a bed.

This was that memorable hour
Which first assured the forced power.

So when they did design
The Capitol's first line,

A bleeding Head, where they begun,
Did fright the architects to run;   70
  And yet in that the State
  Foresaw its happy fate.

And now the Irish are ashamed
To see themselves in one year tamed:
  So much can one man do,
  That does both act and know.

They can affirm his praises best,
And have, though overcome, confessed
  How good he is, how just,
  And fit for highest trust;   80

Nor yet grown stiffer with command,
But still in the Republic's hand:
  How fit he is to sway
  That can so well obey.

He to the Commons' feet presents
A Kingdom, for his first year's rents,
  And, what he may, forbears
  His fame, to make it theirs;

And has his sword and spoils ungirt,
To lay them at the public's skirt.   90
  So when the falcon high
  Falls heavy from the sky,

She, having killed, no more does search
But on the next green bow to perch,
  Where, when he first does lure,
  The falconer has her sure.

What may not then our Isle presume
While victory his crest does plume!
  What may not others fear
  If thus he crown each year!   100

A Caesar he, ere long, to Gaul,
To Italy an Hannibal,
  And to all States not free
  Shall climacteric be.

The Pict no shelter now shall find
Within his particolour'd mind,
  But, from this valour, sad
  Shrink underneath the plaid.

Happy if in the tufted brake
The English hunter him mistake,   110
  Nor lay his hounds in near
  The Caledonian deer.

But thou, the War's and Fortune's son,
March indefatigably on:
  And for the last effect
  Still keep thy sword erect:

Besides the force it has to fright
The spirits of the shady night,
  The same arts that did gain
  A power must it maintain.   120

From *Miscellaneous Poems* (1681)

NOTES TO THE POEMS

BEN JONSON (1572–1637)

Jonson was the stepson of a Westminster master-builder, his
father having died a month before his birth. Educated at West-
minster School, he was taught by the great humanist-anti-
quarian, William Camden,

> to whom I owe
> All that I am in Arts, all that I know.

Subsequently he was employed on miliary service in Flanders,
married a lady whom later he described to his friend, William
Drummond, as 'a shrew, yet honest', and by 1597 had become
an actor-playwright, his first play, *Every Man in his Humour*,
being produced in 1598. In the same year he killed an actor
in a duel, but, claiming 'benefit of clergy', was sentenced only
to imprisonment. While in prison he was converted to the
Church of Rome, to which he adhered during the next twelve
years. His prestige and popularity were greatly enhanced with
the accession of James I in 1603 and the new encouragement
given by the King and his consort to court masques and other
forms of theatrical entertainment, in the composition of which
Jonson proved highly successful. Most of his best work, in-
cluding the four plays *Volpone*, *Epicoene*, *The Alchemist*, and
Bartholomew Fair, were written during the next twelve years
and included in a Folio volume published in 1616. In the course
of his career Jonson enjoyed the friendship and admiration of
many persons of rank and men of letters, the latter including
Shakespeare, Donne, Herrick, Carew, and Suckling. In 1613
he travelled to France as tutor to Sir Walter Raleigh's son, and
in 1618 proceeded on foot to Scotland, where he was entertained
by William Drummond, who in 1619 published notes of their
Conversations, containing Jonson's sharp comments on con-
temporary authors and their works. A disastrous fire, which
destroyed many of Jonson's books and manuscripts in 1623,
was the prelude to a steady decline in his fortunes, further pre-
cipitated by ill-health, poverty, and lack of court favour under

Charles I. He died in 1637 and was buried in Westminster Abbey, where the slab over his grave bears the inscription: 'O rare Ben Jonson'.

Predominant throughout Jonson's writings as in those of many other Renaissance authors, is his conviction of the poet's high prerogative and moral responsibility as a master in the art of 'delightful teaching'. Critical and outspoken, his own apologist in prefaces, epilogues and poetical works, both dramatic and non-dramatic, he does not mince words in censuring his contemporaries where he believes such censure is deserved, at the same time commending with enthusiasm merit where he finds it. His sharp criticisms of Shakespeare in *Discoveries* and *Conversations* are offset by his great poetic eulogy to one whose genius he recognizes as surpassing his own. Though the content and form of his work, dramatic and lyrical alike, are strongly influenced by classical, particularly Latin, writers, his neoclassicism is tempered by a deep sense of native tradition and command of contemporary English idiom and vocabulary, with the result that his best work, even when imitative, seldom smells of the lamp; he reverences the ancients 'as guides, not as commanders'. The effect of this naturalization is amply illustrated throughout the ensuing selection from his shorter poems, which includes pieces from *Epigrams* and *The Forest* (1616), *Underwood* (1640), and songs from the plays.

p. 7 *Inviting a Friend to Supper*

Throughout this poem Jonson draws freely on Martial's *Epigrams*, more particularly from Book XI, Epigram lii, but, as usual, naturalizing his imitation and adapting it to English setting and idiom.

l. 8 *cates:* food. cf. 'Vinum tu facies bonum bibendo' (Martial, V. lxxviii. 16).

l. 10 *salad:* pronounced 'sallet'.

l. 20 *knat, rail, and ruff:* snipe, corncrake, and sandpiper. *my man:* possibly Richard Brome, Jonson's servant, to whom he taught Latin, and who himself became a playwright.

l. 24 *no verses:* cf. 'Plus ego polliceor; nil recitabo tibi' (Martial, XI. lii. 16).

l. 30 *the Mermaid's.* The Mermaid Tavern in Bread Street was frequented by Jonson and his circle of wits.

l. 34 *Luther's beer:* a term of disparagement, paralleled in con-
temporary writings.

l. 36 *Pooly or Parrot:* identified with two informers, possibly
the 'two damn'd villains', who gave evidence against Jonson
at the time of his imprisonment, mentioned in his *Con-
versations with Drummond.*

p. 8 *On My First Daughter*
She died probably between 1595 and 1598, the year of Jonson's
reception into the Roman Church, which may be connected
with the Catholic tenour of the last six lines.

p. 8 *On My First Son*
Benjamin Jonson, 'child of my right hand' (Benjamin in Heb-
rew meaning 'right-handed'), was born about 1596 and died
of the plague in 1603.

p. 9 *An Epitaph on S. P.*
Solomon (spelt Salomon, as in the Vulgate) Pavey died at the
age of thirteen in July 1602, and was buried in the church of
St. Mary Somerset in London. He had performed in Jonson's
Cynthia's Revels and the *Poetaster.*

ll. 15–18 Adapted from Martial's description of Scorpus, a
chariot-driver who died young after winning many prizes.
(*Epig.* X. liii).

p. 10 *To William Camden*
Jonson studied at Westminster school under Camden, the anti-
quary and historian, author of *Britannia*, 1586, and *Annales*,
1615, covering the reign of Elizabeth. In Jonson's *King's
Entertainment* he extols Camden as 'the glory and light of our
kingdom'.

p. 10 *To John Donne*
Jonson told Drummond that he esteemed Donne 'the first poet
in the world in some things', and that he had written all his
best pieces 'ere he was twenty-five years old'.

p. 11 *To Penshurst*
Penshurst was the seat of Lord Sidney, brother of Sir Philip

Sidney, who became Earl of Leicester in 1618. Jonson's eulogy is an early example in English of 'local' poetry, describing an estate or district. Parallel works are Carew's *To Saxham*, Denham's *Cooper's Hill*, and Pope's *Windsor Forest*.

l. 2 *touch:* black granite, used in testing gold on account of its solidity.

l. 10 *Mount:* an elevation in Penshurst Park, still so called.

l. 14 *at his great birth:* on 30 November 1554, the date of Philip Sidney's birth, when an acorn was planted to commemorate the event.

l. 18 *thy Lady's oak.* An old tradition records that a Lady Leicester was taken in travail under an oak tree, thereafter called 'My Lady's Oak' in Penshurst Park.

l. 19 *named of Gamage.* The copse was called 'Lady Gamage's bower', after Barbara Gamage, wife of Lord Sidney, who used to feed the deer there near the entrance to the Park.

l. 26 *Ashore, and Sidney's copse.* Both names are preserved, the first being spelt 'Ashour'.

l. 36 *officiously:* Lat. *officiose*, dutifully.

ll. 48–71: based on Martial, *Epig.* III. lviii. 33–44.

l. 73 *livery:* provision, allowance.

l. 76 *King James.* A room at Penshurst is still called after the King, who stayed there.

l. 77 *the Prince:* Henry, Prince of Wales, who died in 1612.

p. 14 '*Come, my Celia, let us prove*'
This, with the next two songs, addressed to the same lady, are included in *The Forest*, 1616. The first and second are close imitations of Catullus V, 'Vivamus, mea Lesbia, atque amemus,' etc. The first, and ll. 19–22 of the second, had already appeared in 1605 as a song in *Volpone*, preceding an attempted seduction (III. vii).

p. 14 '*Kiss me, sweet: the wary lover*'
l. 13 *Rumney:* Kentish marsh, famous as pasture land.

l. 14 *Chelsey.* According to Norden's *Speculum Britanniae*, 1593, Chelsea is so called 'of the nature of the place, whose strand is like the chesel which the sea casteth up of sand and pebble stones. Thereof Cheselsey, briefly Chelsey, as is Chelsey (Selsey) in Sussex.'

p. 15 *'Drink to me only with thine eyes'*
The theme and images of this, the best-known of Jonson's lyrics, are derived from portions of a letter by the sophist Philostratus (*c.* 170–245 A.D.).

p. 16 *That Women are but Men's Shadows*
According to the *Conversations with Drummond*, this poem was written as a penance imposed upon Jonson by the Countess of Pembroke to 'approve in verse' the premise advanced by her husband, Jonson concurring, that 'women were men's shadows'.

p. 16 *A Hymn to God the Father*
A specimen of Jonson's few religious poems. It was set to music as an anthem by William Crosse and sung in one of the royal chapels. Cf. Herbert, *Discipline*, p. 70.

p. 17 *A Celebration of Charis*
Composed of ten lyrical pieces, written between 1612 and 1623, of which this is the fourth, devoted to the praise of Love and the changing states of the lover and his mistress. The movement and allegorical imagery of Love and his chariot suggest the influence of the masque. The last stanza is incorporated in Jonson's allegorical comedy, *The Devil is an Ass*, II. vi. 94–113.
l. 28 *nard:* aromatic balsam.

p. 19 *On the Portrait of Shakespeare*
Printed with Jonson's name under the portrait of Shakespeare forming the frontispiece to the First Folio edition of his Collected Works, printed in 1623.
l. 8 *writ in brass.* Brass, being harder than pure copper, was used by engravers for printing book-plates.

p. 20 *To the Memory of . . . William Shakespeare*
l. 2 *thy book:* the First Folio edition.
l. 7 *seeliest:* most innocent.
l. 19–21. Alluding to lines in an Elegy on Shakespeare, by William Basse:
> Renowned Spenser, lie a thought more nigh
> To learned Chaucer: and, rare Beaumont, lie
> A little nearer Spenser, to make room
> For Shakespeare in your threefold, fourfold tomb.

l. 31 Perhaps reminiscent of a phrase in Minturno's *L'Arte Poetica*, 1564: 'poco del Latino e pochissimo del Greco'.

l. 35 *Pacuvius, Accius:* obscure dramatists mentioned in Horace's *Ars Poetica*.
  him of Cordova: Seneca.

ll. 36, 37 *buskin, socks:* footwear of actors on the ancient stage, worn for tragedy and comedy respectively.

ll. 37 *shake a stage*, and 69 *shake a lance:* word-play on Shakespeare's name, of a type commonly used by his contemporaries.

p. 22 *To the Noble Lady, the Lady Mary Worth*
Mary, Lady Worth (also spelt 'Wroth'), eldest daughter of Robert, Lord Sidney, and his wife, Barbara Gamage. She married Sir Robert Worth in 1604 and acted in Jonson's *Masque of Blackness* the following year. Jonson dedicated *The Alchemist* to her, as well as two other flattering poems.

l. 3 *exscribe:* copy out.
  your sonnets: appended to Lady Worth's pastoral romance, *Urania* (1621), an imitation of the *Arcadia* of her uncle, Sir Philip Sidney.

l. 6 *numerous:* musical.

l. 14 *ceston:* girdle.

p. 23 From *A Pindaric Ode*
The ode from which this stanza is taken has the regular Pindaric structure, with division into strophe, antistrophe, and epode, Jonson marking these divisions, but translating the terms into English as 'turn', 'counter-turn', and 'stand'. This extract is the third 'turn'. Sir Henry Morison died in 1629, and Sir Lucius Carey, afterwards Lord Falkland, in 1643.

p. 25 *Ode (To Himself)*
This outburst was occasioned by the dismal failure of Jonson's *The New Inn* in 1629. It provoked several replies, one of which, by Thomas Carew, is included in this anthology (p. 80).

ll. 1–10 The 'commission' and 'office' of wit are satirized by Jonson in *Bartholomew Fair* and other works.

l. 22 *Pericles* was printed in 1609, and therefore, by 1629, could be written off as a 'mouldy tale'. Fifteen years earlier, in the Introduction to *Bartholomew Fair*, Jonson had sneered at Shakespeare's late 'romance' plays as 'tales, tempests, and such like drolleries'.

l. 23 *shrieve's:* sheriff's.

l. 33 *orts:* scraps, refuse.

l. 38 *blocks:* moulds.

l. 40 *gilt:* word-play upon 'gilt' and 'guilt'.

l. 45 *nerves:* sinews.

l. 60 A play on the name of King Charles in conjunction with 'Charles's wain' (from 'churl's, or farmer's wain'), a popular name for the constellation of the Great Bear.

WILLIAM BROWNE (1590/1–1643/5)

Born at Tavistock, of Devon descent, Browne was educated successively at Tavistock Grammar School, Exeter College, Oxford, and the Inns of Court. His first collection of poems, *Britannia's Pastorals*, Book I, was published in 1613, *The Shepherd's Pipe*, containing seven eclogues by Browne and four by other poets, in 1614, and *Britannia's Pastorals*, Book II, in 1616. *The Masque of the Inner Temple*, written for performance in January, 1615, was first printed in 1772, and several other works, including an unfinished third book of *Britannia's Pastorals*, remained unprinted until the nineteenth century. In 1624 Browne returned to Oxford as tutor to Robert Dormer, afterwards Earl of Carnarvon, and in 1628 married Timothy, daughter of Sir Thomas Eversfield, after a courtship lasting, apparently, thirteen years. He was well acquainted with contemporary writers, including Jonson, Wither, and Drayton, who numbers him among

> My dear companions, whom I freely chose,
> My bosom friends, and in their several ways
> Rightly born poets.

Of his later years nothing is known, but the record concerning the administration of his estate by his widow shows that he died in or before 1645.

The three collections of Browne's poems published during his lifetime consist entirely of pastorals, avowedly modelled on those of 'Divine Spenser, heaven bred, happy Muse'. Spenserian influence is most conspicuous in *The Shepherd's Pipe*, where themes and verse-forms alike continually recall those of *The Shepherds' Calendar*. *Britannia's Pastorals* consist of a series of bucolic narratives, termed 'Songs', set to heroic couplets, with interspersed lyrics in stanzas. A born lover of nature and rural life, Browne quickens the pastoral convention into poetry, through extensive descriptions, based on close observation of the English countryside, particularly of his native Devon, recounted with metrical fluency characteristic of Spenser and his school. A copy of Browne's pastorals, preserved in the Huth library, contains annotations by Milton, whose early poems, particularly *Lycidas*, suggest several reminiscences from his work.

p. 27 *'Glide soft, ye silver floods'*
Marina, a shepherdess, deserted and disconsolate on the isle of Mona (Anglesey), sees and reads these lines, recording 'A shepherd's moan' on a marble rock 'In characters deep cut with iron stroke'. The lines are an elegiac tribute by Browne to the memory of William Ferrar, who had died young at sea. He was the brother of Nicholas Ferrar, head of the community at Little Gidding, and had contributed a dedicatory poem to the first book of *Britannia's Pastorals*. The elegy, both in language and form, is reminiscent of Spenser, and its influence is clearly reflected in Milton's *Lycidas*.

l. 9 *Thetis:* a sea-goddess, the unwilling wife of Peleus, and mother of Achilles. She lived in the depths of the sea with her father and sisters, Nereus and the Nereids, of whom she was the chief.

l. 11 *plain:* make smooth.

l. 13 *trammels:* braided or plaited locks, from 'trammel', a kind of fishing-net, hence also a hair-net. Cf.

> Her golden lockes she roundly did uptye
> In breaded tramels.
>
> *The Faerie Queene*, II. ii. 15.

l. 22 *shelves:* rocks.

ll. 25–29 *Arion:* a Lesbian poet and musician. Before casting himself into the sea on the command of envious sailors he played his lyre and charmed dolphins, who carried him safely to shore.

l. 38 *calmy*. Cf. 'a still And calmy bay' (*The Faerie Queene*, II. xii. 30).

l. 39 *tell:* count, reckon.

p. 28 '*Venus, by Adonis' side*'
The song is sung by 'a swain of name Less than of worth', to an audience of 'all the western swains', awaiting to entertain, on their arrival, Thetis and her train of Nereids.

p. 29 '*As careful merchants*'
The song is sung by Tavy, the river-spirit, who, having scornfully rejected the wanton advances of the wood-nymphs frequenting his banks, awaits his 'fairest love', Walla, representing the Walla Brook, a stream which, descending over a rocky bed, falls into the Tavy about half a mile above Tavistock. Browne's myth of Tavy and Walla was probably suggested by the story of Egeria, as related by Ovid (*Met.* xv. 482 ff.).

l. 5 Cf. 'Upon a great adventure he was bond' (*The Faerie Queene*, I. i. 3).

l. 21 *Candy:* Candia, i.e. Crete.

p. 30 *Thyrsis' Praise of his Mistress*
Printed in *England's Helicon, or the Muses' Harmony*, 1614.

p. 31 '*A rose, as fair as ever saw the North*'
One of seven 'Visions', clearly imitated from Spenser's *Visions* 'of Petrarch', 'of Bellay' and 'of the World's Vanity' included in his *Complaints* (1591). Each *Vision*, in the form of a sonnet, presents a specific image or instance of prosperity suddenly giving place to disaster, the former being developed in the octave, the latter in the sestet.

p. 32 *Epitaph on the Countess Dowager of Pembroke*
Preserved and ascribed to Browne in a middle seventeenth-century manuscript in the Library of Trinity College, Dublin. The Epitaph was printed, without ascription, in the *Poems* of the Countess's son, William Earl of Pembroke, published in 1660.

l. 3 Sir Philip Sidney wrote *Arcadia* for the benefit of his sister Mary, Countess of Pembroke (*c.* 1561–1621), who may have been partly responsible for additions to *Arcadia*, which, when printed in 1590, bore the title *The Countess of Pembroke's Arcadia*.

l. 10–12 *Niobe*, wife of Amphion, King of Thebes, and mother of twelve children, boasted of her superiority to Leto, the mother of only two, Apollo and Artemis. As a punishment Apollo slew her sons and Artemis her daughters. Their bodies, having lain unburied for nine days, were buried on the tenth by the gods, who out of pity for Niobe's grief changed her into a rock on Mount Sipylus in Phrygia, where she continued to weep.

p. 32 *Song of the Sirens*
The Inner Temple Masque was 'presented by the gentlemen there' on 13 January 1614. The scene at the opening discovers a cliff, upon which are seated two Sirens. One of them sings the first verse, the last two lines of which are repeated by the two together. This is followed by a duel of words between Triton and one Siren concerning the claims to superiority of Tethys and Cynthia as against that of Circe. At the conclusion the Siren resumes her song.

ROBERT HERRICK (1591–1674)

Robert Herrick was born in London, the son of a goldsmith, who died in 1592, suspected of suicide. After a period of apprenticeship to his wealthy uncle, Sir William Herrick, he entered St. John's College, Cambridge, migrated later to Trinity Hall, and took orders in 1623. He accompanied the Duke of Buckingham on an expedition to the Ile de Ré in 1627, and two years later accepted the living of Dean Prior in Devon, which provides the background to much of his poetry. Supporting the Royalist cause, he was ejected from his living in 1648, and in the same year published two volumes of collected poems, *Hesperides* (secular), and *Noble Numbers* (religious). He resided, probably, in London, to which he seems to have paid earlier visits, until 1662, when he returned to Dean Prior, dying there twelve years later. He remained unmarried, but tended by a devoted servant, Prudence Baldwin, and according to Anthony à Wood, the Oxford antiquarian, 'beloved by the neighbouring gentry', notwithstanding his unconventional behaviour, as when, according to one report, he threw his sermon at an inattentive congregation.

Herrick's contacts with London were sufficient to secure him a place within 'the tribe of Ben', of which, as a poet, if not as a personality, he was, in many respects, the liveliest and most versatile member. The great majority of the pieces in *Hesperides* may be classified, broadly, as pastoral and lyrical, though the two kinds, inevitably, overlap; and throughout the collection Herrick quickens and naturalizes many different conventions and forms to a degree unmatched by any of his contemporaries. *The Argument of his Book*, opening the collection, accurately and comprehensively summarizes, within fourteen lines, the diverse aspects of man and nature which have caught his observation and inspired poems ranging in scope and dimension from miniatures like *To Blossoms* and *To Daffodils* to large-scale scenes of rural life like *Corinna's going a Maying* and *The Hock-cart*. As a lyrical poet Herrick, like Jonson, owes much to Catullus and Horace, and his epigrams recall those of Anacreon and the Greek anthology. His treatment of nature and natural phenomena is neither descriptive, like Browne's, nor mystical, like Vaughan's, but idyllic and frankly Pagan, pointing the analogy of nature with human life as a universal process of birth, growth, fruition, and decay. But overriding all other influences in his poetry is the spontaneous impulse, shared with Elizabethan and Jacobean song-writers, inspiring the song that sings itself, the harmonious blending of happy word, phrase, and measure, in which he excels.

p. 34 *The Argument of his Book*
In this opening to his collected poems, a summary of the topics and objects with which they are concerned, Herrick reveals from the outset the piquancy and compactness of his style, attributable largely to his neat assembling of particulars. Within fourteen lines he establishes an essentially English atmosphere and setting, which he maintains consistently notwithstanding his free and frequent use of classical poetry.

l. 3 *hock-carts*, *wassails*, *wakes:* harvest carts, Christmas health-drinking, parish and funeral celebrations.

l. 8 *amber-grease:* a waxy substance, made from whale-sperm and used for perfumes.

l. 9 *times trans-shifting:* the continual passage and movement of time, a basic motive throughout this poem, enforced through allusion to the changing seasons.

p. 34 *Cherry-Ripe*
A street-vendor's cry.

p. 35 *Delight in Disorder*
The motive of 'sweet neglect', illustrated through a succession of diverse objects and attributes and possibly suggested by Jonson's song 'Still to be neat', recurs several times in Herrick's poetry.

> Cf. Thy azure robe I did behold,
>   As airy as the leaves of gold;
>   Which erring here, and wand'ring there
>   Pleas'd with transgression ev'rywhere.
>   *Julia's Petticoat.*

l. 12 *wild civility.* Cf. Next, when those lawny films I see
>   Play with a wild civility.
>   *Art above Nature.*
>   Be she shewing in her dress
>   Like a civil wilderness.
>   *What kind of mistress he would have.*

p. 35 *Corinna's going a Maying*
l. 2 *the god unshorn:* Apollo, the sun-god, frequently represented with rays of light streaming like hair, a symbol of potency. Cf.

> At last the golden Orientall gate
>   Of greatest heaven gan to open faire,
>   And Phoebus fresh, as bridegroom to his mate,
>   Came dauncing forth, shaking his deawy haire.
>   *The Faerie Queene*, I. v. 2.

l. 15 *put on your foliage.* Alluding to the Mayday custom of bedecking houses and their occupants with green.

l. 35 *white-thorn.* Symbolizing both joy and grief.

l. 40 *the proclamation.* Alluding possibly to King Charles's Declaration of 1633, forbidding interference with 'any lawful recreation', including May-games.

l. 51 To 'give a woman a green gown' meant 'to cover her with green by rolling her in the grass', with the secondary implication, 'to deflower her'.

l. 56 Cf. Were beauty under twenty locks kept fast
Yet love breaks through, and picks them all at last.
Venus and Adonis, 575–6.

ll. 57–68 The closest parallels to this particular exposition of the familiar 'Carpe diem' text are Biblical. Cf. *Ps.* XC. 9, *Wisdom*, II. 1–8, and *Prov.* VII. 18.

p. 37 *The Captived Bee: or, the Little Filcher*
l. 23 *scrip:* traveller's wallet or bag.

p. 38 *To the Virgins, to make much of Time*
Earlier literature provides numerous analogues both to the theme of the poem and the imagery through which it is expressed. Cf.

Gather therefore the Rose, whilest yet is prime,
For soone comes age, that will her pride deflowre:
Gather the Rose of love, whilest yet is time,
Whilest loving thou may'st loved be with equall crime.
The Fairie Queene, II. xii. 75.

p. 39 *His Poetry his Pillar*
Assurance of immortality through poetic achievement is a sentiment common to all major Renaissance poets, including Spenser, Shakespeare, Jonson, and Milton. In expressing it Herrick is closely following Horace.

ll. 17–24. Cf.   Exegi monumentum aere perennius,
Regalique situ pyramidum altius;
Quod non imber edax, non Aquilo impotens
Possit diruere, aut innumerabilis
Annorum series, et fuga temporum.
Horace, *Carmina* III. xxx. 1–5.

p. 40 *The Hock-cart*, etc.
The hock-cart was used for carrying home the last load of the harvest. Herrick uses the occasion as subject for an animated picture of rural life and activities, which allows full scope for his artistry in co-ordinating detail with general effect.

l. 9 *maukin:* malkin, a pole bound with cloth at one end, used as an effigy, a scarecrow, or a broom.

l. 21 *cross the fill-horse:* bestride the shaft-horse.

l. 34 *frumentie:* wheat boiled in milk, sweetened, and flavoured.

l. 40 *fanes:* winnowing fans. *fats:* vats.

l. 45 *neat:* cattle.

ll. 49, 50. A Roman, not an English custom. Cf.

> Rusticus emeritum palo suspendat aratrum.
>
> Ovid, *Fasti.* I. 665.

p. 42 *To Primroses filled with Morning-dew*

l. 5 *teem'd:* gave birth to.

p. 43 *To Anthea, who may command him anything*

In this, as in some other love-poems, Herrick may have been influenced by Robert Burton's *Anatomy of Melancholy* (1621), a sub-section of which is devoted to submissiveness on the part of the lover.

l. 2 *Protestant:* protesting, or declaring his devotion.

p. 44 *The Mad Maid's Song*

Character, theme, imagery, and form in combination are strongly reminiscent of the scene of Ophelia's madness in *Hamlet*.

p. 45 *To Blossoms*

l. 1 *pledges:* offspring, by analogy with similar use of Lat. *pignus.*

l. 3 Cf. 'For if they tarry much longer, to say truth they are past date, and no body will respect them'—Burton, *Anatomy of Melancholy.* 3. 2. 5. 5.

p. 46 *His Content in the Country*

l. 4 *my Prew:* Prudence Baldwin, Herrick's housekeeper.

l. 5 *wort:* infusion of malt before fermentation into beer, used probably to mean 'new beer'.

l. 6 *content makes sweet.* Cf. *Eccles.* XL. 18

p. 47 *The Night-piece to Julia*

l. 7 *slow-worm:* used probably for 'adder', though the word is applied normally to a harmless lizard or blindworm.

p. 48 *An Ode for Ben Jonson*
One of four tributes by Herrick to his 'master'.

ll. 5, 6 The names are those of three inns frequented by Jonson
and his 'sons'. The Sun and the Dog have been identified.
'The Triple Tun' has been adapted, presumably to make
a rhyme, from 'The Three Tuns', which was situated on
the Bankside.

p. 49 *His Litany, to the Holy Spirit*

ll. 13–19 Cf.   He has no faith in physic: he does think
                  Most of your doctors are the greater danger,
                  And worse disease to escape.

                              Jonson, *Volpone*, I. iv. 22. ff.

l. 15 *runs on the lees:* is drained to the last drop, 'lees' meaning
the sediment of wine.

l. 25 *the tapers now burn blue:* a sign of the presence of evil spirits.

l. 38 Cf. *Ps.* XXV. 7.

ll. 45, 46 Cf. *Rev.* VI and VIII. 1.

p. 50 *A Thanksgiving to God, for his House*

ll. 7–10 Cf.   we must plant a guard
                  Of thoughts to watch and ward,
                  At the eye and ear, the ports unto the mind.

                              Jonson, *The Forest*, XI. 7–9.

l. 22 *unflead:* unflayed, unaffected by mice or mould.

p. 52 *Grace for a Child*

l. 3 *paddocks:* toads.

GEORGE HERBERT (1593–1633)

The brothers Edward and George Herbert, the former of whom
afterwards became Lord Herbert of Cherbury, a distinguished
philosopher and historian, were scions of a famous Welsh
family. Their father died when George Herbert was only three
years old, and he was brought up by his accomplished mother,
a friend of John Donne. He won distinction at Westminster

School and at Cambridge, where he became successively fellow of Trinity College, Reader in Rhetoric, and Public Orator to the University. Ordained deacon in 1626, he married Jane Danvers in 1628, and in 1629, following ordination as priest, he was appointed rector of Bemerton, near Salisbury. Throughout the three remaining years of his life he attended faithfully to his parish duties, conducting daily services, and frequenting Salisbury Cathedral where, he records, 'his time spent in praying and cathedral music elevated his soul and was his heaven on earth'; he was devoted to music, accompanying his hymns on the lute or viol. He died of consumption in 1633, and was buried beneath the altar of his church. Shortly before his death he entrusted to his friend, Nicholas Ferrar, the manuscript of his collected poems, entitled *The Temple*, which was published and reprinted during the same year. *Herbert's Remains*, which was published and reprinted in 1652, included *A Priest to the Temple*, a manual of rules and instructions for the country parson, and some minor works.

The Temple is a unique monument to the faith, worship, and liturgy of the Anglican Church. Its inspiring motive, intimated by the text on the title-page, 'In this temple doth every man speak of his honour', is developed through a series of about one hundred and sixty short poems, covering all the main aspects and features of the parish church and of the Christian life as promoted within its walls. It includes hymns, miniature studies of the symbolical meaning of church fittings, monuments, and usages (the porch, the windows, the altar, the sacraments, the daily offices and music), commemorations of seasons and festivals in the Christian year, and poems of meditation on the Christian life, its fears and hopes in the warfare between good and evil. Herbert's own personal experience of such spiritual warfare is reflected in many of his poems, for instance *The Storm* and *The Collar*, and referred to by Izaak Walton, who tells us that, at the time of his retirement from Cambridge, 'he had many conflicts with himself, whether he should return to the painted pleasures of a court life, or betake himself to a study of divinity, and enter into sacred orders, to which his dear mother had often persuaded him. These were such conflicts as they only know that have endured them; for ambitious desires, and the outward glory of this world, are not easily laid aside; but at last God inclined him to put on a resolution to serve at His altar.' Contending with the world rather than the flesh, Herbert's conflicts were less violent and more easily resolved than those of Donne, and the prevailing note of his poetry is one of assurance in the power of Divine mercy and redemption to strengthen and perfect human frailty. Sharing the taste of his age, fostered by Donne, for stylistic wit and conceits, he develops it in distinctive ways of his own for the fashioning of emblematic poems, either indented in the shape of the object they describe, as in *The Altar* and *Easter Wings*, or following through progressively an idea or image to a climax, as in *Love*, or *Hope*. But notwithstanding such ingenuities, the simplicity and sincerity of his language and message save his poetry, for the most part, from conveying the effect of artificiality. Other readers, like Herbert's friend, Nicholas Ferrar, may find in *The Temple* 'the picture of a divine soul in every page; and that the whole book was such a harmony of holy passions, as would enrich the world with pleasure and piety'.

p. 53 *The Church Floor*
One of a group of poems in *The Temple* devoted to the structural features and ornaments of the parish church, which Herbert uses as object lessons, showing their spiritual significance. The symbolical interpretation of different features treated in succession recalls the homely manner of the medieval preacher, but the compact, forceful presentation, facilitated through metrical artistry, is peculiar to Herbert.
l. 13 The turn in the argument is emphasized through a corresponding change in the verse.
l. 15 *the marble weeps*. Cf. Virgil, *Geo.* i. 480: 'Et maestum illacrimat templis ebur'.

p. 53 *The Windows*
Here, as in Herbert's hymns and most of his references to music, the emphasis is on Divine 'light and glory', transcending human imperfection, and symbolized in the church.
l. 6 *anneal:* fix in colours, by heating the glass after painting.

p. 54 *The Altar*
In the manuscript and 1633 edition of *The Temple* this poem is

printed in the shape of an altar, as indicated by its metrical form, which became still further emphasized in successive editions up to 1809 through the addition of elaborate engravings. The author of *The Arte of English Poesie* (1589), attributed to George Puttenham, devotes a chapter of his treatise to such poems of 'ocular representation', citing examples both ancient and modern. Herbert's use of the device in *The Altar* and *Easter Wings* is entirely consistent both with his taste for objective symbols and emblems and with the general design of *The Temple*.

l. 4 Cf. *Exod*. XX. 25.

ll. 13, 14 Cf. *Luke*, XIX. 40.

p. 55 *Easter*

The poem, if not specifically designed for musical setting, reflects unmistakably Herbert's musicianship and his familiarity with choral religious music. Though the free verse structure differentiates it formally from that of his hymns, its character, in respect both of theme and language, is essentially hymnic.

l. 5 *calcined:* burnt to powder.

l. 13 *twist a song*. The plaiting of fibres into a cord is applied metaphorically to the interplay of parts in polyphonic music.

l. 15 *three parts vied*. Pursuing the metaphor in l. 13, *vie* meaning either 'to increase by number or addition', or 'to contend with'. The sense, in either case, is that 'heart' and 'lute' need 'spirit' to sustain their three-part music.

l. 24 *perfume*. Associated with the East, and related with 'sweets' (l. 22).

l. 29 *three hundred:* the days of the year in round numbers.

p. 56 *Easter Wings*

Another piece of 'ocular representation' (cf. *The Altar*), in this case applied to successive phases of meditation, with appropriate imagery, on the message of Easter. The extreme simplicity of the language and the correspondence between the evolution of thought and the verse-pattern combine to modify, if not entirely to efface, the effect of artificiality. The shaping of the stanzas is analogous to that of alternating *diminuendo* and *crescendo* in a musical score, matching parallel phases in thematic development.

l. 10 *the fall*. The paradox of *felix culpa*, advanced by St. Augustine, that Adam's sin was 'happy' in occasioning the glorious Redemption by Christ is familiar in medieval writings and is embodied in the text of the office for the Easter Vigil.

l. 19 *imp*. A term in falconry, meaning to engraft feathers on a damaged wing, thus restoring power to fly.

p. 56 *Redemption*

A sonnet, constructed in a form typical of Herbert, evolving as an allegory in phases divided evenly over three stanzas to an abrupt, unexpected dramatic climax in the concluding couplet. Characteristic likewise is the speaker's sense of intimate personal relationship with God. The homely speech and imagery, as in many of Herbert's poems, follow a long tradition of preaching and homiletic literature.

p. 57 *Jordan*

The first of two poems bearing this title in the 1633 edition. Of the several suggested explanations of the title, probably the most satisfactory is that of F. E. Hutchinson, who sees an allusion to Elisha's counsel to Naaman, the Syrian leper, to 'Go and wash in Jordan seven times . . . and thou shalt be clean' (II *Kings*, V. 10).

ll. 6–10 The censure is directed against two distinct kinds of artificiality in contemporary poetry, first the pastoral convention with its 'enchanted groves' and 'purling streams', secondly stylistic ingenuity and wit, 'Catching the sense at two removes'. Herbert may well have had in mind Sidney's protests against

> You that do search for every purling spring,
> Which from the ribs of old Parnassus flows,
> And every flower (not sweet, perhaps), which grows
> Near there about, into your poems wring,
> You that do dictionary method bring
> Into your rimes, running in rattling rows.
>
> *Astrophel and Stella, XV*

protests repeated in other sonnets of the same cycle and in *An Apology for Poetry*. It must, none the less, be admitted that in this respect both Herbert and Sidney alike to some degree stand self-condemned.

l. 7 *sudden arbours:* arbours appearing suddenly, causing surprise, which for long was esteemed a virtue in horticulture.

l. 12 *pull for prime:* draw a card, which makes the player 'prime', a term in the game of primero, said to have been introduced into England by the suite of Catherine of Aragon.

p. 57 *Avarice*

A sonnet in thematic and metrical structure similar to *Redemption*, though with a different rhyme-scheme.

p. 58 *The World*

l. 7 *balconies.* Spelt in the original edition *balcones*, from the Italian *balcone*, a trisyllabic word, stressed on the second syllable.

l. 11 *sycamore.* Associated, by false etymology, with the fig-tree.

l. 14 *summers:* horizontal bearing beams, supporting joists or rafters.

p. 59 *Virtue*

The poem conforms with a thematic pattern frequently followed by Herbert, the turn of thought, showing the significance of the title, being held in reserve until the last stanza.

l. 5 *angry:* red, having the colour of an angry face.

l. 10 *sweets:* perfumes.

l. 11 *closes:* cadences, a musical term.

l. 15 *coal:* cinders, or ashes, to which the whole world turns in death, contrasted with 'season'd timber', which remains alive.

p. 59 *Unkindness*

l. 1 *coy:* backward, reserved.

l. 16 *pretendeth to:* aspires to, is a candidate for.

p. 60 *Life*

Vaughan quotes the whole of this poem in *The Mount of Olives* (1652), a devotional work, with the preliminary commendation: 'Hark how like a busy bee he hymns it to the flowers, while in a handful of blossoms gather'd by himself, he foresees his own dissolution.'

l. 15 Based on the belief that the rose acts as a purge.

p. 61 *The Quip*

The theme, savouring of medieval morality drama, may refer specifically to Herbert's experiences of inner conflict between the claims of God and of Mammon prior to his ordination. The references to the speaker's taste for music, quick wit, and conversation are clearly personal.

l. 2 *train-bands:* trained bands, the civic military force of London.

l. 19 *an Oration.* Possibly an ironical allusion to Herbert's former office as Public Orator in Cambridge, which would give additional piquancy to the double rhyme.

l. 24 *home:* an adverb, 'directly'; cf. 'to drive a nail *home*'. The monosyllabic last word lends additional force to an already powerful close.

p. 62 *Hope*

A tour-de-force of compression and multiple symbolism, each of the symbols being open to different interpretations. The *watch* given to Hope suggests the giver's wish that his hope may be realized within a definite time, the *anchor* he receives in return advising him that he must hold on longer. The *old prayer-book* witnesses to long and regular devotion, the *optic*, or telescope showing that the answer to prayer may be a distant prospect, or discernible only by faith. The *vial full of tears* could symbolize either self-pity or repentance, *a few green ears* immaturity, a further counsel to wait and be patient. Despairing of hope fulfilled on earth, the speaker fastens his hope on eternity, symbolized in the *ring* of unity with God.

p. 62 *Time*

Herbert's apparent resignation to the prospect of death, doubtless intensified through ill-health, is reflected both in the theme of the poem and the light, half-serious tone with which it is sustained.

p. 63 *Peace*

ll. 22, 23 Melchisedec, King of Salem, who 'brought forth bread and wine' (*Gen.* XIV. 18) is described as 'king of peace' in *Heb.* VII. 2. Herbert represents him as typifying Christ.

p. 65 *The Storm*

l. 6 *object:* place before them, making them conscious of their guilt.

l. 7 Stars have their meteor-showers, though high above us they appear untroubled.

p. 65 *The Pilgrimage*

A profoundly personal poem, with autobiographical overtones, notwithstanding the agelong familiarity of the theme—the allegorical pilgrimage—and of the conventional personifications associated with it.

l. 14 *the wold.* An allusion to the wolds of Lincolnshire, which Herbert would have known from visiting his sister Frances. Possibly 'wold' is intended to pun with 'would'.

l. 17 *one good angel.* A pun on the gold coin thus named. Some have supposed that Herbert may be referring to his marriage to Jane Danvers, the 'friend' being her kinsman, Harry Danvers, Earl of Danby, with whom Herbert lived for a time.

p. 67 *The Collar*

One of the most impassioned of Herbert's poems concerned with spiritual conflict, the violent fluctuations of mood and feeling being reflected in continuous free verse. The language represents his nearest approach to that of contemporary tragedy. It is worthy of note that the collar, a figure of discipline, symbolizing the motive force of the poem, appears only in the title.

l. 6 *in suit:* in service to another.

p. 68 *The Pulley*

The pulley, likewise confined to the title, signifies God's methods of drawing man towards himself, man's restlessness being subordinate to a divine scheme. Herbert has also made use of the story of Pandora, the first mortal woman. Jupiter gave her a box filled with blessings of the gods, but when it was opened they all slipped out except Hope, which lay at the bottom.

l. 15 *both:* both God and man.

p. 69 *Aaron*

Grierson compares the reiterating final words and rhymes with the swelling and dying sound of a bell.

ll. 1–3 Aaron's priestly garments, described in *Exod*. XXVIII, included a mitre with a gold plate engraved with the words 'Holiness to the Lord'.

l. 18 *striking:* as the clapper strikes the bell.

p. 70 *Discipline*

Both in language and form this poem strongly resembles Ben Jonson's *Hymn to God the Father*; see p. 16.

p. 71 *The Elixir*

This poem was revised several times, to its advantage, before the final version as printed in 1633. The elixir signified 'the philosopher's stone', reputed to turn base metals into gold.

l. 7 *prepossest:* having the prior claim.

l. 15 *tincture:* a supposed spiritual principle, or immaterial substance, whose quality may be infused into material things.

l. 23 *touch*. The word was used for testing gold by rubbing it with the touchstone.

p. 72 *Love*

One of the most satisfying of Herbert's poems. Within the compass of eighteen lines it illustrates the distinctive excellencies of his finest work: sincerity of conviction and motive inspired by a personal faith, power to express this conviction in language at once simple and intense, and poetic imagination, enlivened by quick inventiveness in dramatic presentation, and controlled by masterly overall command of structure and form.

THOMAS CAREW (1594/5–1640)

Thomas Carew, the son of Sir Matthew Carew, Master in Chancery, was born either in Holland, or at West Wickham, in Kent, and completed his education at Merton College, Oxford, and the Middle Temple. In 1613 he joined the service of Sir Dudley Carleton, a relative by marriage, whom he accompanied to Italy and the Hague, but in 1616 was dismissed from his post for slander. Between 1619 and 1624 he was employed on diplomatic service under Sir Edward (later Lord) Herbert, subsequently 'followed the court before he was of it', becoming gentleman of the privy chamber in 1628, and sewer in ordinary to Charles I in 1630. His wide circle of acquaintance included Jonson, Suckling, and other prominent men of letters. His great elegy on Donne was included in a collection of Donne's poetry published in 1633, and *Coelum Britannicum*, a masque, based on dialogues of Giordano Bruno, was produced at court, with a setting by Inigo Jones, in 1634, and published in the same year. Carew took part in the 'Bishops' War' of 1639 and died in the following year. The first edition of his collected poems appeared at about the time of his death.

Lord Herbert of Cherbury, in his Autobiography, speaks of 'Thomas Carew, that excellent wit', and Clarendon, the historian, terms him 'a pleasant and Facetious wit'; the more puritanical Izaak Walton, however, esteems him 'a poet of note and a great libertine in his life and talk'. Both Clarendon and Walton refer specifically to Carew's death-bed repentance, of which further evidence is provided in his paraphrases of psalms, written towards the end of his life. His poems as a whole are characterized by the frank sensuality and expressive brilliance common to all the Caroline courtly poets, and reflect the influence of both Jonson's humanism and of Donne's meta-physical wit. Carew's conscious artistry, more palpable than Jonson's, is shrewdly hit off by Suckling in *A Sessions of the Poets*:

'His muse was hard-bound, and th'issue of 's brain

Was seldom brought forth but with trouble and pain.'
But the trouble and pain are used to full advantage in the two poems addressed to his two masters, the one containing the most judicious assessment of Donne's poetry by any of his contemporaries, the other a frank yet balanced criticism of the great Ben's merits and failings alike, such as few of his 'tribe' dared to offer, and none to better effect.

p. 73 *The Spring*
An early example of a type of generalized descriptive poetry which became increasingly popular during the later seventeenth and eighteenth centuries. The ironic contrast between nature in

springtime and the lover slighted by a cold mistress is a favourite convention used by Renaissance poets from Petrarch downwards, including Elizabethan song-writers; but Carew's immediate source, particularly at the opening and the close of the poem, is probably Ronsard's *Amourette*.

l. 3 *candies:* coats with ice.

l. 6 *sacred birth.* Swallows were sacred to the Penates (household gods), as noted by Sir Thomas Browne in *Pseudodoxia Epidemica*. It is unnecessary to accept, with some editors, a manuscript reading 'second' for 'sacred'.

l. 13 *Now all things smile.* Cf. Virgil *Eclog.* vii. 55: 'Omnia nunc rident'.

p. 73 *To A.L.: Persuasions to Love*
Counsel to increase is another favourite theme of erotic poetry, as notably, though addressed to a man, in the first group of Shakespeare's *Sonnets*. Lines 1–26 of Carew's poem are original, followed by a transitional couplet, the remainder being a free translation from a canzone, *Belleza caduca*, by the popular Italian poet, Giambattista Marino (1569–1625). As three manuscript versions end at l. 26, this portion may originally have been written as an independent poem. A manuscript version of ll. 37–48, with an autograph musical setting by Henry Lawes, is still extant.

p. 76 *To my Mistress sitting by a river's side. An Eddy*
The motive figure of this poem, announced in the title, derives from Donne's *Elegy VI* (ll. 21–34). Carew uses it again in a memorial poem on the Earl of Anglesey, addressed to his widow:

> He chose not in the active stream to swim,
> Nor hunted Honour, which yet hunted him.
> But like a quiet eddy, that hath found
> Some hollow creek, there turns his waters round (ll. 57–60).

p. 77 *Song. To my Inconstant Mistress*
This and the following poem strike the note of cynical disillusion recurrent in the erotic poetry of Wyatt, Donne, and several of Carew's contemporaries. Classical analogues are to be found in Catullus and Propertius.

p. 77 *Disdain Returned*

The first two stanzas of this poem were printed during Carew's lifetime in Walter Porter's *Madrigals and Airs* (1632). The last, generally thought to be inferior and omitted in some anthologies, may have been composed later.

l. 19 *power*: supernatural power.

p. 78 *To my Mistress in absence*

ll. 9, 10: the figure suggests comparison with Lovelace's *To Lucasta, Going beyond the Seas*, and Donne's *Extasy*, but Carew's mundane desires are far removed from Donne's Platonic idealism.

p. 79 *Epitaph on the Lady Mary Villiers*

The last, and best, of three epitaphs on the same child, probably the daughter of Christopher Villiers, Earl of Anglesey, one of Carew's patrons. Her burial at the church of St. Martin in the Fields is registered under the date 4 August 1630.

p. 80 *To Ben Jonson*

l. 6 The decline in Jonson's dramatic power following *The Alchemist*, which accounts for the failure of his later plays, has been generally recognized.

l. 11 *all thy eaglets*. Eagles were said to test their young by making them gaze at the sun, driving from the nest any that flinched.

l. 18 *By city-custom or by gavel-kind*: legal terms, defining the equal division of estate after death among dependants, the former applying to London, the latter more specifically to Kent.

l. 31 *Goodwin*: the treacherous Goodwin sands, off the coast of Kent.

l. 35 *To theft the blood of martyred authors*: a pungent reference to Jonson's notorious imitations and plagiarisms.

l. 48 *verge*: strictly, an area within the jurisdiction of the Lord High Steward, extending to a distance of twelve miles round the King's court.

p. 81 From *An Elegy upon the Death of the Dean of Paul's, Dr. John Donne*

This extract forms the conclusion to one of the finest of Carew's

poems, consisting of ninety-eight lines, of outstanding import-
ance as a unique critical appreciation of Donne and his achieve-
ment by a contemporary poet and disciple. Like his poem
addressed to Jonson, it shows critical penetration, quickened
through succinct expression in verse. The *Elegy* was first
printed, along with several others, in the 1633 edition of
Donne's collected *Poems*.

JOHN MILTON (1608–1674)

The son of John Milton, a London scrivener and an amateur
composer, Milton was born in Bread Street, Cheapside, on 9
December 1608. He was educated at St. Paul's School, and from
1625 to 1632 at Christ's College, Cambridge, where he was
known as the 'Lady of Christ's', and wrote *At a Vacation
Exercise* (1628), *On the Morning of Christ's Nativity* (1629), the
sonnet '*On Arriving at the Age of Twenty-Three*' (1632), and the
epitaph on Shakespeare prefixed to the Second Folio edition of
1632. *L'Allegro* and *Il Penseroso* were probably written either
while Milton was still at Cambridge or shortly after he went
down. Between 1632 and 1638 Milton resided at his father's
house in Horton, Bucks., engaged in private study and writing.
The works belonging to this period include two masques—
Arcades, presented before the Countess Dowager of Derby at
Harefield, and *Comus*, with music by Henry Lawes, produced
at Ludlow Castle before the Earl of Bridgewater in 1634—and
Lycidas, contributed to a collection of elegies, published in 1638,
on Edward King, a distinguished young member of Christ's,
who had been drowned in the Irish Channel the previous
summer. During 1638 and 1639 Milton travelled in France and
Italy, where he consorted with Italians and their academies,
meeting Galileo in Florence. On his way home, learning of the
death of his friend, Charles Diodati, he wrote a Latin elegy in
his memory, entitled *Epitaphium Damonis*, printed privately.
Having returned to London, for a time he taught a few private
pupils. The outbreak of the Civil War put an end for the time
being to his projects as a poet, and during the next twenty years
his literary work was practically confined to controversial

pamphlets. In 1643 he married Mary Powell, the seventeen-year-old daughter of an Oxford gentleman, who left him a month after their marriage but returned two years later. Subsequently he contracted two other marriages in 1656 and 1663. The failure of the first resulted in the publication of Milton's divorce pamphlets, and their sequel, *Areopagitica* (1644), an attack on the licensing of the press, the most famous of his prose works. A collection of his poems was published in 1645 and a second issue with additions, which contains all the poems included in this anthology, in 1673. In 1649 he was appointed Latin Secretary to the Parliamentary Committee on Foreign Affairs, and three years later became totally blind. His life, after the Restoration, was comparatively uneventful, but it was during this period that he completed and published his major works, *Paradise Lost* in 1667, reprinted with additions in 1673, and *Paradise Regained* with *Samson Agonistes* in 1671. He died on 8 November 1674, and was buried in St. Giles, Cripplegate.

Milton's poetry, unlike his prose, is detached, to an exceptional degree, from the impact of current affairs and society, deriving its inspiration primarily from his inner life and genius, quickened through wide and devoted scholarship. Two of his prose works, *The Reason of Church Government* and *An Apology for Smectymnuus*, contain autobiographical passages of the greatest value and significance in throwing light upon his upbringing and ideals, and many passages in his poetry reflect his feelings and state of mind at the time when they were composed. But specific references to his friends and interests are confined to his Latin juvenilia and a few of the sonnets, apart from which all his works are on religious or moral themes, 'sage and serious', as he describes Spenser.

Unlike most of his contemporaries, he was little influenced either by Jonson or by Donne, deriving more from Spenser and his successors, including William Browne. Of his careful artistry we fortunately have first-hand evidence, as the manuscripts of some of his poems, in his own handwriting, are still preserved in Trinity College, Cambridge. Viewed as a whole, Milton's work represents the finest and most comprehensive embodiment in English poetry of Christian humanism, which developed at the Renaissance through the blending of Christian and classical culture, a basic motive in the *Nativity Ode*, fostered subsequently, as Milton himself avers, through prolonged study at home and abroad. His acute sense of form, perceptible throughout his poetry and monumentally represented in *Lycidas*, derives from the humanistic principle of imitation, whereby execution after a pattern becomes an end in itself, specific borrowing or reminiscence from earlier poets merely providing raw material for a new creation.

Milton's affinity with earlier humanists and his acceptance of their ideals appear likewise in his lofty sense of vocation as a dedicated poet, himself 'a true poem; that is, a composition and pattern of the best and honourablest things', endowed with the poet's prerogative as a seer or prophet, and 'soaring in the high region of his fancies, with his garland and singing robes about him'.

p. 83 *On the Morning of Christ's Nativity*

Begun at dawn on Christmas Day, 1629, as Milton states in his sixth Latin Elegy, addressed to Charles Diodati. The heavy, long-lined stanza of the Introduction contrasts with the lighter, lyrical measure of the Hymn, each form of stanza ending with a Spenserian alexandrine.

l. 10 *wont:* past tense of wone, to dwell.

l. 23 *wizards:* wise men. Cf. drunkard, sweetard (sweetheart).

l. 28 *touch'd with hallow'd fire:* Cf. *Isaiah*, VI. 6, 7.

l. 41 *pollute:* polluted, Lat. pollutus.

ll. 45–52 The allegorical image suggests reminiscence of the contemporary masque. Cf. ll. 141–148.

l. 48 *the turning sphere:* refers to the Ptolemaic theory of the universe, which represents the earth as a fixed body at the centre of eight concentric revolving globes.

l. 51 *myrtle wand.* The myrtle, sacred to Venus, was the emblem of love.

l. 64 *whist:* silent. Cf.

> Curtsied when you have and kiss'd
> The wild waves whist.
>
> *The Tempest.* I. ii. 379.

l. 68 *birds of calm:* halcyons, fabled to calm wind and wave during their breeding time at the winter solstice.

l. 71 *influence:* an ethereal fluid, believed to flow from the stars, affecting human destinies.

l. 88 *than:* alternative spelling for then, current in Milton's day and used for the sake of the rhyme.

l. 89 *Pan:* applied to Christ, as in Spenser's *Shepherds' Calendar*, 'May', 54, and 'July', 49.

l. 92 *silly:* innocent.

l. 116 *unexpressive:* inexpressible.

ll. 119–122 Cf. *Job*, XXXVIII. 7.

l. 125 referring to the Ptolemaic notion of music made by the moving spheres.

ll. 158, 9 Cf. *Exodus*, XIX. 16.

l. 168 *The old Dragon:* Cf. *Rev.* XX. 2.

l. 172 *swinges:* lashes.

l. 173 ff. *The oracles*, etc. Plutarch, in *De Defectu Oracularum*, 17, gives a graphic account of the cessation of oracles and the announcement of the death of Pan at a time which Christian writers identified with that of the Crucifixion. The story is related in the Gloss to *The Shepherds' Calendar*, 'May', 54, from which Milton probably derived it. It is noteworthy that Milton is less violently hostile to classical heathen deities than to those of the Old Testament.

l. 191 *Lars and Lemures:* household gods and goblins.

l. 197 *Peor and Baalim*. Peor was the name of a mountain, and Baal a Phoenician word used for 'god' generally, with plural 'Baalim'. 'Baal-Peor', in *Psalm* CVI. 28, and elsewhere in the Old Testament, means 'the god of Peor', but Milton apparently supposed it to refer to two separate deities.

l. 199 *that twice battered god:* Dagon, the fish god of the Philistines, whose idol fell down twice before the Ark of the Covenant set in his temple. I *Sam.*, V. 2–4.

l. 200 *mooned Ashtaroth:* Hebrew plural of Astarte, the Phoenician nature goddess representing the female principle. Her star was the planet Venus, and she was possibly regarded also as a moon-goddess. Her classical equivalent was Venus-Aphrodite.

l. 203 *The Lybic Hammon*: Amun, an Egyptian god, whose emblem was a ram.

l. 204 *Thammuz:* Tammuz, the Syrian equivalent of Adonis, according to legend slain by a boar but annually coming back to life after his blood had flown afresh, the event being celebrated by mourning and rejoicing. The myth symbolizes the alternation of summer and winter.

l. 205 *Moloch:* a Semitic sun-god, worshipped and pacified through human sacrifice by fire.

l. 211 *brutish gods of Nile:* Egyptian deities, most of which were represented by beasts or their attributes, Isis, the chief goddess having the horns of a cow, and her two sons, Horus and Anubis, respectively the head of a hawk and the head of a jackal.

l. 213 ff. *Osiris:* the Egyptian creator and almighty judge, whom Milton identifies with the bull-god Apis, worshipped at Memphis. His brother Set, the Greek Typhon, shut him in a chest, which was thrown into the Nile. Isis regained the chest, but later Typhon found it and tore the body of Osiris into fourteen pieces, which he scattered on the ground.

l. 226 *snaky twine.* Typhon was sometimes represented as a serpent.

l. 240 *youngest teemed:* youngest born.

p. 90 *On Time*
Composed probably about 1630, and headed in the Trinity College MS. 'to be set on a clock case'. The metrical form, as in *At a Solemn Music,* probably adapted from that of the Italian canzone or madrigal, is composed basically of iambic pentameters, with interspersed lines of three feet and concluding with an alexandrine. The result is a highly effective small-scale specimen of Milton's 'apt numbers', in other words the flexibility of his language and verse as modulated to his theme.

l. 3 *plummet's:* weight's.

l. 12 *individual:* indivisible.

p. 91 *On Shakespeare*
Dated 1630, and printed in the Second Folio of Shakespeare's works in 1632.

l. 1 *What:* why.

l. 4 *star-ypointing:* a spurious archaism, after the manner of Spenser, the *y-* being a traditional prefix of the past, not of the present participle.

l. 8 *live-long: lasting* in the Second Folio version.

l. 11 *unvalu'd:* invaluable.

ll. 13, 14 Shakespeare makes us marble with thinking too much by reading him, and thus deadening or weakening our 'fancy'. The closing lines are in keeping with the monumental character of the poem and of the inscription for which it was intended.

p. 92 *Sonnet*

Written on Milton's twenty-third birthday. A draft in Milton's own hand is extant in a prose letter to a friend preserved in the Cambridge manuscripts and stating his reasons for not hurrying to enter a profession. The concluding lines suggest a deep sense of vocation, so far undefined.

l. 4 *shew'th:* rhyming with 'youth' and 'truth', thus indicating the contemporary pronunciation of 'shew'.

ll. 5, 6: possibly referring to his youthful appearance, implied also in his nickname 'the Lady of Christ's'.

p. 92 *At a Solemn Music*

Dated 1630 conjecturally by Masson, who translates the title '*At a Concert of Sacred Music*'. The printed text compared with the drafts in the Cambridge manuscripts shows several revisions. Milton inherited a love of music from his father, who composed and published sacred music and madrigals.

l. 1 *Sirens.* According to Plato and other authorities, a siren sat on each of the revolving heavenly spheres, producing music.

l. 6 *content:* the reading of the 1645 edition. 'concent' (1672), i.e. 'harmony', may be preferred.

l. 7 Cf. *Ezek.*, I. 26.

l. 23 *diapason:* originally the interval of the octave, containing all the notes in the scale, here applied to the seven days' work of creation.

l. 28 This line was revised seven times before Milton finally adopted it as printed.

p. 93 *L'Allegro*

This and *Il Penseroso* are companion studies of contrasted moods or types of character, the cheerful active with the thoughtful contemplative. There are no drafts of them in the Cambridge manuscripts, and it has generally been assumed that Milton wrote them while living at Horton. The syllogistic character of the two contrasted themes savours of the academic exercise such as Milton might have undertaken while still at Cambridge.

ll. 1, 2 The representation of Melancholy as the child of Midnight and the hell-hound Cerberus is Milton's invention.

l. 10 The Cimmerians in Homer are described as a people living beyond the ocean in a land of eternal darkness. Subsequently the name was applied to an historical people, living near the Black Sea.

l. 12 *Euphrosyne:* one of the three Graces, signifying cheerfulness. Her sisters were Aglaia (brightness) and Thalia (bloom). Generally they are represented as daughters of Zeus, but Milton, for his present purpose, derives her alternatively from Bacchus (wine) and Venus (love), or from Aurora (dawn) and Zephyr (the west wind).

l. 27 *cranks:* literally crooks or bends, applied to verbal turns or conceits.

l. 28 *becks:* signs with the finger or head.

l. 29 *Hebe:* daughter of Zeus and Hera, and goddess of youth, represented by Homer as cupbearer to the gods.

l. 40 *unreproved:* probably 'unreprovable', or innocent.

ll. 45, 46 In fairness to Milton's powers of observation, even though he may have seen nature 'through the spectacles of books', 'to come' must clearly be referred not to the lark, but to the speaker who comes to his window and bids good morrow to his neighbours.

l. 45 *in spite of:* in defiance of.

l. 48 *eglantine:* dog-rose or honeysuckle, the usual meaning being sweetbriar.

l. 67 *tells his tale:* probably 'tells his story', but possibly 'numbers his flock', as Warton suggested.

l. 71 *lawns:* wide open spaces.

l. 75 Cf. the opening of the last song in *Love's Labour's Lost:* 'When daisies pied and violets blue.'

l. 77 *Towers and battlements:* referring, perhaps, to Windsor Castle, near Horton.

l. 80 *Cynosure:* the constellation of the Lesser Bear, hence a guiding star or centre of attraction.

ll. 83–88 Milton is applying to English rustics names from traditional pastoral poetry, more specifically from the Eclogues of Virgil.

l. 94 *rebeck:* an old-fashioned type of fiddle.

l. 102 *Faery Mab.* She made dreams come true, and stole cream. Cf. Mercutio's description of her in *Romeo and Juliet*, I. iv. 54 ff.

l. 104 'And by the Friar's lantern led' is the reading of the second edition, which cannot be fitted to the syntax of the lines that follow. Assuming the first reading to be correct, 'by Friar's lantern led' must be in parenthesis, 'led' referring to 'he'.

Friar's lantern: Jack-o'-the-Lantern, or Will-o'-the-Wisp, possibly confused by Milton with Friar Rush, domestic spirit.

l. 105 *the drudging Goblin:* Robin Goodfellow, Hobgoblin, Shakespeare's Puck, a domestic sprite, alternately helpful and mischievous, with a partiality for cream.

l. 108 *shadowy:* having been used during the night.

l. 110 *lubber fiend.* A lubber was a servant employed for the baser duties of the house. 'Lob of spirits', applied to Puck, comes from the same root.

l. 117 *please us then:* through reading and reflection at home, after a day out of doors in company with rustics.

l. 125 In Jonson's masque *Hymenaei* Hymen, the god of marriage, made his entry clad in a saffron-coloured robe and carrying a torch.

l. 132 *sock:* comedy, the sock being the low-heeled shoe worn by actors in comedy. For tragedy the shoe was high-heeled and called 'buskin'.

ll. 133, 134 The contrast between Jonson's learning and Shakespeare's 'sweetness', 'fancy', and 'wood-notes wild' is sufficiently pertinent; in each case 'L'Allegro', in keeping with his role, confines his attention to comedy.

l. 136 *soft Lydian airs.* In ancient Greek music there were three basic modes, Dorian, Phrygian, and Lydian, the last being associated with sweetness and effeminacy.

ll. 151, 152 Cf. If these delights thy mind may move,
      Then live with me and be my Love.
Marlowe, *The Passionate Shepherd to his Love*, 27-28

p. 97 *Il Penseroso*

The contrived antithesis with *L'Allegro* is established through the personifications of the opening lines, and subsequently maintained through reference to the setting and time of day and to the speaker's occupation and reflections, enforced by means of natural description and imagery.

l. 3 *bestead:* avail.

l. 10 *pensioners of Morpheus:* bodyguard of the god of Sleep. The term 'pensioners' was applied to a bodyguard established by Henry VIII.

l. 16 *O'erlaid with black.* Etymologically melancholy means 'black bile'.

l. 18 *Prince Memnon's sister.* Memnon, according to legend, was a beautiful Ethiopian prince, who fought on the side of the Trojans and was killed by Achilles. Though he had sisters, there is no record that one of them was likewise beautiful, so this is probably Milton's invention.

ll. 19–21 Cassiope, the wife of Cepheus, King of Ethiopia, and mother of Andromeda, challenged the Nereids for the superiority of her, or her daughter's, beauty. In revenge Poseidon sent a sea-monster to ravage the country, and Andromeda was offered in sacrifice, but rescued by Perseus. Subsequently Cassiope was raised to heaven and transformed into the constellation Cassiopeia; hence *starred*.

ll. 23–30 Milton invents a mythological origin for Melancholy, as he does for Mirth, representing her as the daughter of Saturn by his child Vesta, goddess of the domestic hearth. The epithet 'solitary' may perhaps be attributed to the fact that Saturn was the oldest of the Latin gods, and may have been supposed to share the gloomy 'saturnine' disposition of his Greek counterpart, Cronos.

l. 29 *Ida's inmost grove:* a cave on Mount Ida in Crete, where Zeus (Jove) as an infant was hidden from his father.

l. 31 *pensive nun:* perhaps pursuing the reference to Vesta, reverenced as patroness of the sacred fire tended by Vestal virgins.

l. 33 *grain:* originally scarlet dye, later signifying colour generally.

l. 35 *cypres lawn:* black crepe.

ll. 51–53 Cf. *Ezek.*, X. Milton for his own purpose boldly personifies one of the four cherubs surrounding the sapphire throne as Contemplation.

l. 55 *hist:* a verb, from the interjection, either 'summon noiselessly', or 'move, saying "Hush!" '.

l. 59 The chariot of Cynthia, the moon-goddess, was drawn by horses, cows, or mules. Milton probably has confused it with that of Demeter, which was drawn by dragons.

l. 60 *the accustomed oak:* the oak over which I generally see her.

l. 65 *I walk unseen:* contrast 'walking not unseen', *L'Allegro*, 57.

l. 77 *the air:* the state of the weather.

l. 87 *out-watch the Bear:* watch until sunrise, since in the Northern Hemisphere the Bear never sets.

l. 88 *thrice-great Hermes:* Hermes Trismegistus ('thrice-greatest'), a description of Thot, the Egyptian Hermes, god of wisdom, the reputed author of the sacred books termed Hermetic, most of which were, in fact, written by Neo-Platonic writers of the third or fourth centuries.

ll. 88, 89 *unsphere The spirit of Plato:* bring back the disembodied spirit of Plato through studying his works.

l. 93 *dæmons.* Plato conceived of dæmons as agents between God and man, every man having an attendant dæmon. The division, implied by Milton, of dæmons into four classes, corresponding with the four elements, was a medieval notion.

ll. 97–102 In contrast with *L'Allegro*, associating comedy with the work of Jonson and Shakespeare, *Il Penseroso* identifies 'gorgeous tragedy' with that of the Attic poets, paying only lip-service to the 'rare' work of a 'later age'.

l. 104 *Musæus:* a semi-mythical poet, said to be the son of Orpheus. A few fragments attributed to him are still extant.

ll. 109–115 Referring to Chaucer's *The Squire's Tale*, which was left unfinished.

l. 113 *virtuous:* having magical properties.

ll. 116–120 Clearly alluding to the poetry of Spenser, possibly also to that of Ariosto and Tasso.

l. 123 *trick'd and frounced:* dressed up and curled.

l. 124 *the Attic Boy:* Cephalus, the lover of Eos (Morning).

l. 130 *minute drops:* falling at intervals of a minute. Cf. 'minute-guns'.

l. 141 *garish:* staring.

l. 156 *pale:* enclosure.

l. 157 *high-embowed:* with high arches.

l. 158 *massy-proof:* proof against massive weights.

l. 159 *storied:* depicting a story.

p. 102 *'Sweet Echo, sweetest Nymph'*
On the title-page of the first edition, printed in 1637, *Comus* is
described as 'A Masque, presented at Ludlow Castle, 1634,
before the Earl of Bridgewater, Lord President of Wales'. The
plot, based upon a well-known story from English folk-lore,
concerns the capture of a Lady, lost in a wood, by an enchanter,
Comus, and her rescue by her two brothers. Milton applies to it
an allegorical significance by figuring in the persons of the Lady
and Comus chastity and lust. In the original performance the
parts of the Lady and her brothers were played by the Earl's
three children, the Lady Alice Egerton, Viscount Brackley, and
Mr. Thomas Egerton. Milton's friend, Henry Lawes, who com-
posed the music, played the part of the Attendant Spirit. The
Song, sung by the Lady, follows the conclusion of her opening
speech in which, having heard the noise of Comus and his
fellow-revellers, soliloquizing on the possible fate and where-
abouts of her brothers, she avows her assurance in the power of
chastity.

l. 1 *Sweet Echo.* In Jonson's *Cynthia's Revels* Echo, who figures
       as one of the characters, is invoked in somewhat similar
       terms by Mercury in the opening scene.
l. 2 *thy airy shell:* the hollow vault of the atmosphere.
l. 3 *Meander's margent green.* Meander, a river in Asia Minor,
       well known for its numerous windings (hence 'meander-
       ing'), may have been chosen on this account as a suitable
       abode for Echo.
l. 8 *thy Narcissus.* Echo pined away for love of Narcissus till
       only her voice was left; for punishment Narcissus was made
       to fall in love with his own shadow and afterwards was
       transformed into the flower narcissus.
l. 12 *Parly:* speech.
       Daughter of the Sphere. Probably Daughter of the Atmos-
       phere, or Air. Cf. *At a Solemn Music*, l. 2:
       Sphere-born harmonious sisters, Voice and Verse.

p. 103 *Lycidas*
Dated November 1637 and entitled 'Lycidas' on the original
draft in the Cambridge manuscript; printed at Cambridge the
following year, in a collection of poems inscribed to the memory
of Edward King, by some of his colleagues. There is no evidence

of Milton's friendship or close acquaintance with King, *Lycidas* being rather a masterly poetic monument, compounded of traditional pastoral conventions and expressing the author's convictions and ideals.

l. 1 *Yet once more:* a traditional opening in earlier poetry, but possibly implying that Milton had not written English verse since the composition of *Comus* three years before. *Laurels, myrtle* and *ivy* are all emblems both of poetry and of mourning.

l. 2 *never sere:* never dry, evergreen.

l. 4 The first of several interspersed short lines of three feet, a device which Milton had already used in *At a Solemn Music;* the elegiac effect in *Lycidas* is highly successful.

l. 7 *compels:* singular, as the two subjects express one idea.

ll. 8, 9 *Lycidas.* The name occurs in the eclogues of Theocritus, Moschus, and Virgil. The figure of repetition is common in pastoral elegies.

ll. 10, 11 Some of King's poems, all in Latin, are extant, but none is of any considerable value.

l. 15 *the sacred well:* the Pierian spring at the foot of Mount Olympus in Thessaly, the original birthplace of the Muses, or possibly the fountains Aganippe and Hippocrene on Mount Helicon, to which their worship was later transferred.

l. 21 *as he passes, turn.* The Muse is masculine, standing for the poet.

ll. 23–26 Milton and King had been contemporaries at Christ's College, Cambridge, but the extent of their intimacy may be exaggerated by the former in accordance with pastoral convention.

l. 28 *gray-fly:* 'the dor-beetle' is suggested by the O.E.D.

l. 34 Satyrs and Fauns had the bodies of men and the lower limbs of goats. The reference is evidently to fellow-students in Cambridge and to a don, styled Damœtas (l. 36), this name occurring in the sixth *Idyll* of Theocritus and the third *Eclogue* of Virgil.

l. 45 *canker:* caterpillar.

l. 46 *taint-worm.* According to Sir Thomas Browne the 'taint' was a small red spider, supposed to infect cattle.

ll. 50, 51 The interrogative apostrophe is adapted from Theocritus and Virgil.

l. 52 *the steep:* possibly Penmaenmawr, in Carnarvonshire, opposite Anglesey.

l. 53 *the famous Druids.* Druidic circles in this neighbourhood had already been surveyed in Milton's time.

l. 54 *Mona:* Anglesey.

l. 55 *Deva:* the Dee, near the mouth of which, at Chester, King embarked on his fatal voyage.

ll. 58–63 Orpheus, the son of the Muse Calliope, was torn to pieces by Thracian maenads in one of their Bacchanalian orgies. The Muses collected the fragments of his body and buried them at the foot of Mount Olympus, but his head, having been thrown into the river Hebrus, was carried to the island of Lesbos, and buried there.

ll. 67–69 Amaryllis and Neæra are imaginary names, drawn from Virgil's eclogues. 'To sport' may signify either 'to make love' literally, or 'to write frivolous love poetry'.

l. 75 Milton confuses the Furies with the third of the three Fates. Clotho spun the thread of a man's life, Lachesis wound it, and Atropos cut the thread at the end.

l. 77 *my trembling ears:* referring to the popular superstition that tingling of the ears is a sign that one is being talked about.

l. 79 *foil:* a thin plate of metal, set under a jewel in order to display it, or 'set it off'.

ll. 85, 86 The fountain Arethusa, in the island of Ortygia off Syracuse, is invoked as the Muse of Sicilian pastoral poetry practised by Theocritus; and Mincius, a tributary of the Po, because Virgil, the chief Latin pastoral poet, was born and lived near it.

l. 88 *my oat proceeds:* a return from the strain of a 'higher mood' to the oaten pipe of rustic pastoral.

ll. 89, 90 Triton, the Trumpeter of the Waves, comes on Neptune's behalf to inquire into the cause of the disaster.

l. 96 *Hippotades:* Æolus, god of the winds, son of Hippotes.

l. 99 *Panope:* a Nereid, or sea-nymph.

l. 103 *Camus:* god of the Cam, on which Cambridge stands.

l. 106 *sanguine flower:* hyacinthus, more probably dark blue larkspur than the modern hyacinth, supposed to have sprung from the blood of Hyacinthus, a beautiful youth beloved by Apollo who accidentally killed him with a quoit.

l. 109 *The Pilot:* St. Peter, entrusted with the keys of heaven
and hell, and represented as Chief Shepherd of the Flock.

l. 111 *amain:* with force.

l. 113 *How well could I have spared.* King had intended to take
Holy Orders.

ll. 116–131 In his bitter attack on the Anglican clergy under
the primacy of Archbishop Laud, Milton follows the pre-
cedent of Spenser, who attacks the clergy of his time,
though with less violence, in *The Shepherds' Calendar.*

l. 124 *scrannel:* feeble, reedy.

l. 128 *the grim wolf:* the Church of Rome, ever in wait to make
converts.

l. 130 *that two-handed engine.* The several strained interpre-
tations of this image which have been suggested are more
ingenious than convincing. 'Two-handed' clearly means
'wielded by both hands', and 'engine' may be applied to
any heavy weapon. There is a suggestion of the exe-
cutioner's axe, but no more specific application. Milton's
intention of threatening the clergy with impending punish-
ment, however, is made clear from a preliminary note in
the 1645 edition to the effect that in this monody the author
'by occasion foretells the ruin of our corrupted Clergy, then
in their height'.

l. 132 After the polemic interlude and the passing of the 'dread
voice' of St. Peter, the poet returns to the pastoral strain,
invoking Alpheus, the lover of Arethusa and united with
her in the fountain of Ortygia.

l. 136 *use:* dwell, as in 'used' meaning 'accustomed'.

l. 138 *the swart star:* the dog-star, Sirius, in the ascendant
during the summer and therefore associated with a dark,
or suntanned complexion.

ll. 142–151 An impressionistic and poetic description, in keep-
ing with the monumental character of the elegy and not to
be judged by the criterion of scientific accuracy. There are
many precedents and analogues, particularly in pastoral
poetry.

l. 142 *rathe:* early, surviving in the comparative degree in
'rather'.

l. 143 *crow-toe:* applied both to the wild hyacinth and to the
buttercup.

l. 144 *freaked:* streaked.

l. 146 *woodbine:* honeysuckle.

l. 149 *Amaranthus:* an imaginary unfading flower, its genus including prince's feather and love-lies-bleeding.

l. 151 *laureat hearse:* tomb or coffin, bedecked with the poet's laurel.

l. 160 *Bellerus old.* Apparently an invention by Milton, personifying Bellerium, the Roman name for Land's End. In the Cambridge manuscript the name is 'Corineus', that of the mythical founder of Cornwall according to early chroniclers.

l. 161 *the guarded Mount:* St. Michael's Mount in Mount's Bay, Cornwall, with a craggy seat overlooking the sea associated with an apparition of St. Michael during the fifth century.

l. 162 *Namancos and Bayona's hold:* the tower of Namancos and the castle of Bayona, near Cape Finisterre, both marked in the old maps of Milton's time.

ll. 163, 4 *Look homeward, Angel,* etc. Addressed first to St. Michael, and then to the dolphins, who had borne Arion, the musician, safely to shore after he had thrown himself overboard.

l. 168 *the day-star:* the sun.

l. 183 *the Genius of the shore:* the *numen,* or tutelary stream; a renewed note of Paganism after the Christian conclusion.

ll. 186–193 For the epilogue, spoken ostensibly in Milton's own person, the impassioned style of the mourner is abruptly dropped, giving place to one more equable, restrained, and colloquial. The contrast is enforced through the metrical change from flexible rhymed couplets, broken in places by unrhymed lines, to a formal eight-lined stanza, composed of three alternating rhymed lines and a concluding couplet.

p. 109 *On the late Massacre in Piedmont*
Written in 1655 following the persecution of the Waldensian community in the Piedmontese Alps after their refusal to obey an edict of the Duke of Savoy, ordering them either to abandon their properties and leave his dominions, or to become Roman Catholics. Strong letters of protest, addressed to the Duke of Savoy and other European potentates by Milton, as Latin Secretary, on behalf of Cromwell, are still extant. As the result of these and other remonstrances the edict was withdrawn.

l. 10 *Their martyred blood and ashes sow.* Reminiscent of a
    famous pronouncement of Tertullian: 'The blood of the
    martyrs is the seed of the Church'.
l. 12 *the triple Tyrant:* the Pope, so called from his three-tiered
    crown.

p. 109 *On his Blindness*
Milton became totally blind in 1652 or 1653, and this sonnet
was probably written shortly after. He refers to his blindness in
two later sonnets, addressed to Cyriack Skinner, in his prose
pamphlets, and in an intensely moving autobiographical passage
at the opening of *Paradise Lost*, Book III.
l. 3 *that one talent.* Referring to the parable of the talents in
    Matt. XXV. 14–20.

SIR JOHN SUCKLING (1609–1642)

The son of Sir John Suckling, successively Comptroller of the
Household and Secretary of State, Suckling was born at Whitton
in Middlesex, and educated at Trinity College, Cambridge, and
Gray's Inn. Inheriting considerable wealth on the death of his
father, in 1627, he travelled abroad during the next three years,
was knighted on his return, in 1630, and, having served for a
short time under Gustavus Adolphus in Germany, returned
home again in 1632. Thereafter he lived the life of a wealthy
Cavalier, on intimate terms with Thomas Carew, Richard Love-
lace, and other courtly wits, whose characters and vagaries
form the substance of his satire *A Sessions of the Poets*, circulated
in manuscript. His play *Aglaura*, lavishly produced at his own
expense, was printed in 1638, and at about the same time he
wrote a religious work, *Account of Religion by Reason*. On the
outbreak of the Scottish campaign, in 1639, he provided a troop
of a hundred horse which, along with other Royalist forces,
was defeated by Lesley. He sat in the Long Parliament as
member for Bramber, but being implicated in a plot to rescue
Strafford, he fled to France, where, according to the antiquary
John Aubrey, he committed suicide.

'Natural, easy Suckling', as Millamant describes him in *The*

Way of the World, was an early and a distinguished repre-
sentative of 'the Mob of Gentlemen who wrote with Ease' during
the reigns of Charles I and Charles II. Of himself in *A Sessions of
the Poets* he confesses that he

'prized black eyes, or a lucky hit
At bowls above all the trophies of wit.'

The prevailing gallantry and good humour of his poetry is
tempered by a sharp, satiric wit, ranging from light raillery to
pungent cynicism and materialism, which reflects the influence
of the *Libertin* school of French poets. In common with most of
his English contemporaries, he was an admirer of both Jonson
and Donne, and their influence is reflected in some of the
selections which follow; but his work shows little trace of either
Jonson's erudition or Donne's intellectualism, seeming, in the
words of Edward Phillips, Milton's nephew, 'to savour more of
the grape than the lamp'. Many of his lyrics, for which he is
chiefly remembered, were composed as songs and set to music.
In a class of its own is his English Epithalamium, *Ballad of a
Wedding*, a masterpiece of 'occasional' poetry, where the gay,
dancing measure provides a perfect accompaniment to hilarious
description and comment.

p. 110 *A Ballad upon a Wedding*
It has traditionally been assumed that the occasion of the ballad
was the marriage of Roger Boyle, Lord Broghill, to Lady
Margaret Howard, daughter to the Earl of Suffolk, in January
1641. An alternative, more recent suggestion refers it to the
marriage of Lord Lovelace in July 1638, partly on the ground
that Suckling wrote another poem, *Upon my Lord Broghill's
Wedding*. Suckling has effectively naturalized the conventional
epithalamium by adapting it to an English domestic scene,
enlivened by hilarious description and characterization, and
setting his theme to a traditional English verse-form.

l. 7 *Charing Cross*. The party proceeds from Charing Cross to
    the church of St. Giles in the Fields.
l. 8 *sell our hay:* the site of the present Haymarket, where hay
    was sold until the early nineteenth century.
l. 9 *a house with stairs:* possibly Suffolk House, later Northum-
    berland House, on the site of the present Northumberland
    Avenue.

l. 19 *course-a-park:* a game in which a girl cried out and was chased.

l. 32 *Whitsun-ale:* a dancing ceremony held at Whitsuntide.

pp. 114, 115 *Sonnets I and II*

During the sixteenth and early seventeenth centuries the term 'sonnet' was not restricted to poems of fourteen lines, but loosely applied to lyrical poems, more particularly those of a reflective character, of different lengths and metrical patterns. In common with all Suckling's love-poems, the 'Sonnets' express a cynical and materialistic attitude to love, similar to that of the French *Libertin* poets.

p. 114 'Of thee, kind boy'

I. l. 10 *cozenage:* deception.

p. 115 'O for some honest lover's ghost'

II. l. 1 The opening line recalls that of Donne's *Love's Deity:* 'I love to talk with some old lover's ghost', and the note of parody is maintained throughout the poem.

l. 23 *Sophonisba.* Daughter of Hasdrubal, affianced to Masinissa, king of the Numidians, but forced to marry Syphax, prince of western Numidia, in order to be saved from captivity. She was a favourite tragic heroine in sixteenth- and seventeenth-century drama.

ll. 26–28 Philoclea, Pyrocles, and Amphialus are characters in Sidney's *Arcadia.*

p. 116 *Why so pale and wan?*

The most famous of Suckling's lyrics, from his tragedy *Aglaura,* IV. i.

p. 117 *Against Fruition*

Another typical instance of cynical realism and calculation characteristic of Suckling, as of other contemporary court lyrists, carried to further extremes by wits of the Restoration period. The abrupt opening recalls the 'shock tactics' of Donne.

p. 118 *Upon My Lady Carlisle*

A dialogue between Suckling and his friend, Thomas Carew, whose contrasted attitudes and reactions towards the lady they are watching spotlight the difference between sacred and profane love. Lady Carlisle, wife of the first Earl, James Hay, numbered among her admirers several poets, including, besides Suckling and Carew, Herrick and Waller.

p. 120 *Song*
The basic figure round which the song revolves recalls Sidney's poem in *Arcadia* beginning 'My true love hath my heart, and I have his', but the development reads more like a parody, substituting slick word-play for Sidney's idealistic reflections, with corresponding changes in form.

RICHARD CRASHAW (1612/3-1649)

The son of the Rev. William Crashaw, a distinguished theologian of strong anti-Papistical views, Richard Crashaw was born in London and educated at the Charterhouse, subsequently at Pembroke College, Cambridge, becoming a fellow of Peterhouse in 1636. At Cambridge he was attracted towards the High Church Laudian party, and became acquainted with the poets Joseph Beaumont and Abraham Cowley. He was also intimate with Nicholas Ferrar and the religious community at Little Gidding. In 1643, following the outbreak of the Civil War, he was deprived of his fellowship and sought refuge abroad. In the course of the next two years he was in Holland and in Paris, where he met Cowley and other exiles, including Queen Henrietta Maria and the Countess of Denbigh. Having joined the Roman Church, he proceeded, with introductions from the Queen, to Rome, and after a phase of severe poverty and neglect, entered the service of Cardinal Pallotta, who, finding him 'a man of angelical life', in 1649 secured him a post at Loretto, where he died shortly afterwards.

Epigrammatum sacrorum liber, a collection of Latin poems by Crashaw, appeared in 1634, when he was still at Cambridge. In 1646, after his exile, a collection of his religious and secular poems in English was published under the title *Steps to the, Temple, Sacred Poems. With the Delights of the Muses*, reissued with additions, in 1648. A final selection of his sacred poems, inscribed to the Countess of Denbigh, 'in hearty acknowledgement of his immortal obligation to her goodness and charity', appeared in 1652, three years after his death.

The range of Crashaw's culture was exceptionally wide, embracing practical knowledge of Italian and Spanish as well as of classical languages and literature, besides skill in music, painting, and engraving; and this versatility is well represented in his poetry. As a metaphysical poet he has more in common with Cowley than with Donne, but derives most from the works of Spanish and Italian poets and mystics of the Counter-Reformation, whose influence is widely perceptible in his choice of sacred themes, the impassioned fervour of his devotional apostrophes, and the 'fine excess' of his 'baroque' imagery and style. In phases of spiritual ecstasy inspired by contemplation on Christ or the Saints, his reach is apt to exceed his grasp, poetry collapsing into bathos; but at his best, as in the closing lines of the *Hymn to Saint Theresa*, he attains a high level of lyrical power, inspiring other poets, particularly those of his own faith such as Francis Thompson and G. M. Hopkins. On other levels, as illustrated in *Wishes to his (Supposed) Mistress* and the lines addressed to the Countess of Denbigh, he shows his command of familiar, natural style and compact expression, adapted alike to the play of wit and fancy and to the serious exercise of persuasive argument.

p. 121 *Wishes to his (Supposed) Mistress*
Included in *The Delights of the Muses*, 1648, having already appeared, in a shorter form, in *Wit's Recreations*, an anthology published in 1641.
l. 21 *rampant:* obtrusive, showy.
l. 40 *oppress:* overwhelm, i.e. surpass.
l. 42 A Harleian MS. reading contemporary with Crashaw gives this line as 'Themselves in simple nakedness', and has been adopted by some editors.
l. 64 *bin:* are.
l. 70 *flight:* fleeting.
ll. 88, 89 *Sydnæan showers*, etc. Referring to the 'sweet discourse' of Sir P. Sidney, more specifically in *Arcadia*.

p. 125 From *The Flaming Heart*
The title is identical with that of an English translation of St.

Theresa's *Autobiography*, published in 1642. As first published in 1648, the poem consisted of eighty-four lines of rhapsodic apostrophe, descending not infrequently into bathos, upon a picture of the saint with a seraph beside her. The passage quoted in this anthology was added in a later version published in 1652, the first eight lines serving to connect the earlier part with the inspired peroration that follows, from line 9 onwards, which represents Crashaw's poetic power at its highest level.

St. Theresa of Avila (1515–82) wrote many mystical works, including her *Autobiography*. Crashaw had already published in 1646 *A Hymn to the Name and Honour of the admirable Saint Teresa*, acclaiming her, in a preliminary note, as 'a woman for angelical height of speculation, for masculine courage of performance, more than a woman'.

p. 126 *To the Countess of Denbigh*

A fine example of epistolary poetry, a form seldom adopted by Crashaw. It was published in *Carmen Deo Nostro*, 1652, and in an enlarged version, entitled *A Letter from Mr. Crashaw to the Countess of Denbigh*, the following year. Its power and persuasiveness spring from the strength of the poet's conviction, communicated with the aid and subtle use of emblematic imagery, and the presentation of his argument in easy, familiar style.

Susan, Countess of Denbigh, was sister to George Villiers, the celebrated Duke of Buckingham, and accompanied the Queen in exile to France, where, probably, she made Crashaw's acquaintance. She was received into the Roman Church, but the date of her reception is unknown.

l. 2 *stands trembling*. The basic idea underlying this image and others related to it in the poem is anticipated in one of Crashaw's earlier epigrams.

p. 128 *Charitas Nimia*

Alike in theme and style reminiscent of Herbert rather than of Crashaw's favourite models. Catholic baroque imagery is confined to lines 19–29.

p. 131 *An Epitaph*

An altered and extended version, published in 1652, of a piece first published in 1648, the chief addition being lines 11–14.

RICHARD LOVELACE (1618–1657)

The eldest son of Sir William Lovelace, a member of a Kentish family, Richard Lovelace is believed to have been born at Woolwich in 1618, though this is not certain. He was educated at the Charterhouse and at Gloucester Hall, Oxford, where he was registered as M.A. in 1636. His life as a courtier and country gentleman was interrupted by the 'Bishops' War' of 1639–40, in which he took part, subsequently presenting to Parliament the so-called 'Kentish Petition', asking for the restoration of Bishops and of the Anglican liturgy. The petition was burnt by the common hangman, and Lovelace was confined for a time in the Gatehouse, Westminster, remaining, after his release, a prisoner on parole. He joined the King at Oxford in 1645, and in 1646, having raised a regiment for the French King, took part in the French campaign, and was wounded at Dunkirk. Returning to England, he was again imprisoned in 1648, and in the following year published a volume of collected poems entitled *Lucasta: Epodes, Odes, Sonnets, Songs, etc.* Of his last years virtually nothing is known, but Anthony à Wood, the Oxford historian, states that he was reduced to poverty, and died wretchedly in Gunpowder Alley, London.

The fame of Lovelace rests mainly upon a few of his lyrics, addressed to 'Althea' and 'Lucasta'. While some of his poems sound a note of chivalric idealism recalling Sidney and other Elizabethans, he shares the cynicism fashionable among courtly poets of his time, though this is less conspicuous in Lovelace than in Suckling. He appears to have been a versatile connoisseur and patron of the arts, his associates in London including the poet Andrew Marvell, the painter Peter Lely, and the musician Henry Lawes. His poetry suggests erudition and studied art, as instanced in *The Grasshopper*, where, like Jonson, he refurbishes to new purpose material gleaned from classical poets. He resembles Jonson likewise in his care for structure and formal compactness. He was not unaffected by the metaphysical fashion, which misled him from time to time into using laboured comparisons and, in Dr. Johnson's phrase, 'heterogeneous ideas, yoked by violence together'. But at his best, as in *Gratiana*, he withstands the dangers of studied artifice, maintaining effective counterpoint between theme, imagery, and form.

p. 132 *To Lucasta, Going beyond the Seas*
Set to music by Henry Lawes (1596–1662), who composed music for Milton's *Comus* and Carew's *Coelum Britannicum* as well as for many songs by seventeenth-century poets.

p. 133 *To Lucasta, Going to the Wars*
This song was set to music by John Laniere, a member of a distinguished musical family, but the setting is lost. It is impossible to say which of the several wars in which Lovelace was engaged is referred to.

ll. 10, 11 : the change from the formal 'you' to the familiar 'thee' may be intentional.

l. 12 *Honour:* a play on the double meaning of military honour and chastity.

p. 133 *Gratiana Dancing and Singing*
A fine example of lyrical integrity and evolution. The dual imagery of dancing and cosmic movement develops to a climax in the last stanza, where song and dance are matched with the music of the spheres.

p. 134 *The Scrutiny*
One of the most popular of Lovelace's songs, included in Cotgrave's *Wit's Interpreter*, 1655, set to music by Thomas Charles, and printed in Playford's *Select Musical Ayres, and Dialogues*, 1652. The frank admission and defence of promiscuity are typical of 'the mob of gentlemen who wrote with ease' in 'either Charles's days', as they were termed by Pope.

p. 135 *Princess Louisa Drawing*
Princess Louisa was the daughter of the King of Bohemia, and granddaughter of James I. She was taught painting by Gerard Honthorst. Lovelace probably met her at the Hague, as she was acquainted with the Gorings.

ll. 7–9 Cupid betrayed Echo, as Narcissus, 'her delight', did not return her love.

ll. 14–17 Syrinx, fleeing from Pan's embraces, was transformed into a reed, from which he fashioned his pipe, subsequently named after her.

ll. 18–21 Ariadne, daughter of Minos, king of Crete, was ravished by Theseus, and abandoned on the island of Naxos.

l. 19 *wafts:* beckons.

ll. 22–25 Anaxarete scorned the love of Iphis, who hanged himself.

l. 27 Leucothoë's father buried her alive on hearing of her love affair with Apollo.

l. 28 Daphne, beloved and pursued by Apollo, was changed by her mother into a laurel tree.

p. 137 *The Grasshopper*
Mr. Charles Cotton, a poet for whose marriage Lovelace wrote *The Triumphs of Philamore and Amoret*, where he is described as 'noblest of our youth, and best of friends'. Cotton wrote lines on Lovelace's death, and was the friend of Izaak Walton, adding a second book to *The Compleat Angler*.

l. 3 *Drunk every night.* Grasshoppers 'have a certain sharp pointed thing in their breast . . . and with it they suck and lick in the dew'. (Pliny's *Natural History*, in Philemon Holland's translation).

l. 12 *streams:* may be read either as a verb, 'streams away' (Grierson), or as a noun, forming with 'men' and 'thyself' the object of 'mak'st merry'.

l. 17 *verdant:* ironic word-play on the green of ice and of grass.

l. 23 *this cold Time:* alluding probably to the political situation.

l. 33 *Night as clear Hesper.* The evening star shines most brightly at the approach of night, 'so will our tapers whip Night from the lighted casements of the room where we amuse ourselves, and, by stripping her black mantle from the dark Hag, put everlasting day in the place of Night' (Wilkinson).

l. 37 *untempted:* unattacked.

p. 138 *To Althea, from Prison*
The best known and most popular of Lovelace's songs, written probably during his imprisonment in the Gatehouse in 1642, and first published in *Lucasta* seven years later. It was included in several eighteenth-century anthologies, including the *Reliques* of Percy, who used a manuscript copy. Robert Bell, in his *Lives*

of the Most Eminent Literary and Scientific Men of Great Britain,
1839, said of it 'there is scarcely any single production of the
seventeenth century which enjoys such extensive popularity.'

p. 139 *Love Enthroned*
Included in the posthumous collection of Lovelace's *Poems,*
published in 1660.

HENRY VAUGHAN (1622–1695)

Henry Vaughan, 'Silurist', as he calls himself, from 'Silures',
the early inhabitants of Wales, belonged to an old Breconshire
family, and was born at Newton St. Bridget, on the banks of the
Usk, from which he derived the name 'Olor Iscanus' for one of
his poems and for the collection which it opens. After a private
education, he was entered with his twin brother, Thomas, at
Oxford, probably at Jesus College, in 1638, but left after two
years for London, where, having begun to study law, he aban-
doned this for medicine, which he practised subsequently for a
time in Brecon. Soon after the outbreak of the Civil War, he
served for a time with the Royalist forces. The earliest published
volume of his collected poems appeared in 1646 under the title
*Poems, with the Tenth Satire of Juvenal Englished; Silex Scin-
tillans,* a collection of religious poems, was published in 1650,
and re-issued, with the addition of an introduction and a second
part, in 1655. *Olor Iscanus,* a miscellany of dedications, elegies,
and translations, appeared in 1651; and *Thalia Rediviva,* con-
sisting of both sacred and secular pieces, including some by
Thomas Vaughan, in 1678. Henry Vaughan appears to have been
married twice, first to Catherine Wise, of a Warwickshire family,
and, after her death, to her sister Elizabeth. Of his later years
nothing substantial is known, but we have a record of his death
and burial at Llansantffraed in 1695.

Silex Scintillans, which contains the finest of Vaughan's
poems, followed a spiritual conversion, which, according to his
own statement in the preface to the 1655 edition, was directly
inspired by the works of 'the blessed man, Mr. George Herbert,
whose holy life and verse gained many pious converts, of whom

I am the least'. It is not, therefore, surprising to find throughout the collection many direct borrowings from Herbert in titles, themes, phrasing, and style. But notwithstanding such affinities, the two poets differ fundamentally both in outlook and in culture, as might be expected from their different environments and hereditary backgrounds. Vaughan's religious faith is sustained and strengthened, not, like Herbert's, primarily through religious practice or the concrete symbols of worship and sacrament, but through a deep and overwhelming sense of the Divine presence pervading the cosmos, and perceptible in every natural object. His poetry is strongly influenced by the contemporary Christian Platonism treated systematically in the mystical and hermetic writings of his brother, Thomas.

The central motive of *Silex Scintillans*, intimated by its title, 'the flashing flintstone', is the state of fallen man, oppressed through sin and corruption, but reaching outward and upward aspiring to capture his heritage in the eternal world of light. In *Affliction* sickness is represented as 'the great elixir, that turns gall To wine and sweetness', *Corruption* figures primeval man while still retaining 'some glimpse of Eden', *The Retreat* and *Childhood* extol 'angel infancy', driving 'white designs', still spying 'some shadows of eternity'. External nature, which supplies a basis to many of Vaughan's poems and a source for much of his imagery, he treats habitually as the symbol of God's presence in an ordered universe, and the bond between the created world and its Creator. *The Morning Watch* celebrates the dawn awakening 'In sacred hymns and order, the great chime, And symphony of nature', *The Waterfall* is a reflection upon God's purifying grace, *The World* presents an exalted vision of cosmic eternity, 'Like a great ring of pure and endless light'. Though Vaughan's treatment of nature is reflective and analytic rather than descriptive, and rarely localized, viewed as a whole it conveys the general effect of the Breconshire countryside in which he spent most of his life, and features in his language and prosody show affinities with Welsh poetry. His poetry is more complex and less controlled than that of Herbert, and when moralizing on familiar themes he is apt to become turgid and diffuse. He is at his best when least trammelled by the things of this world, and most purely absorbed in contemplation of the next.

p. 141 *To Amoret gone from him*
Included in *Poems, with the tenth Satire of Juvenal Englished*,
1646,the first published collection of Vaughan's poems. Amoret
may stand for Catherine Wise, Vaughan's first wife; but
this is uncertain. The poem, though conventional and reminis-
cent of Donne, illustrates Vaughan's characteristic treatment of
nature and its overtones of mysticism.

l. 9 *the wanton eddies.* Cf. the figure in Carew's *To my Mistress
    sitting by a river's side*, p. 76.

l. 20 *influence:* used in an astrological sense, the stars being
    supposed to influence human lives and affairs. This and
    the following lines recall Donne's *A Valediction forbidding
    mourning.*

l. 22 *element their love:* are the elements of their love, or give
    substance to it. Cf.

> Dull sublunary lovers love
>   (Whose soul is sense) cannot admit
> Absence, because it doth remove
>   Those things which elemented it.
>   Donne. *A Valediction forbidding mourning.*

p. 141 *The Retreat*
The theme anticipates that of Wordsworth's *Ode on the Inti-
mations of Immortality*, and the possibility that Wordsworth was
influenced by Vaughan is strengthened by the fact that his
library contained a copy of *Silex Scintillans*. Seventeenth-
century analogues are Herbert's two poems entitled *Holy
Baptism*, and Earle's *Character of a Child*, which opens *Micro-
cosmographie*, 1628.

l. 6 *a white, celestial thought.* Vaughan's frequent use of white-
    ness as a symbol of purity is an instance of his 'Welsh
    English', *gwyn* in Welsh having the multiple meaning
    white, fair, happy, holy, and blessed.

l. 8 *my first love.* Cf. *Rev.*, II. 4. 'Nevertheless I have somewhat
    against thee, because thou hast left thy first love', and
    Vaughan's *Corruption*, 7.

l. 20 *shoots of everlastingness.* The same phrase is applied to
    Conscience, having 'the character of a God stamped in it',
    by Owen Felltham in his essay 'Of the Soul', *Resolves*, 1628.

l. 26 *city of palm trees.* Cf. 'Jericho, the city of palm trees',
    Deut., XXXIV. 3.

p. 143 *The Morning Watch*

The title, like many of Herbert's, suggests a canonical act of devotion.

l. 1 *O joys! infinite sweetness!* Cf. 'O Book! infinite sweetness!' Herbert, *The Holy Scriptures*, I.

l. 8 *bloods:* an active verb, 'supplies blood to'. Vaughan appears to be combining both the old and new physiology, the former teaching that blood was 'begotten' of the heart, the latter Harvey's recently propounded theory of circulation.

ll. 18, 19 *Prayer is The world in tune.* Taken directly from Herbert's *Prayer:* 'A kind of tune, which all things hear and fear', though the cosmological figure of 'the great chime And symphony of Nature' is Vaughan's characteristic addition.

ll. 33, 34 Referring possibly to the covering of live embers at night for rekindling the next day's fire.

p. 144 *Corruption*

There are several parallelisms between this poem and *Magia Adamica*, by Vaughan's twin brother, Thomas, particularly in their portrayal of the contrast in man's state and attitude before and after the Fall.

l. 25 *leiger.* An ambassador-*leger* or *lieger* is a permanant, ordinary as opposed to an extraordinary ambassador. *Leger* is derived from Anglo-Saxon *liegan*, 'to lie', and has no connection with 'legate'.

l. 40 Cf. *Rev.*, XIV. 14, 15.

p. 145 *Affliction*

This title was used by Herbert for no less than five poems. Vaughan's treatment of the theme is largely independent of these, but clearly influenced throughout by his knowledge of medicine and experience as a physician. The argument is based on the philosophical notion that the permanence of every kind of being is maintained through change.

l. 4 *the great elixir:* red tincture, one of the two goals of alchemy, credited with the property of renewing life, the other being the philosopher's stone, for transmuting base metals into gold. Both are combined and given religious significance by Herbert in *The Elixir*.

l. 37 *tuning his breast:* cf. Herbert, *The Temper* (I):
>   This is but tuning of my breast
>   To make the music better.

p. 146 *The World*

An allegorical vision, inspired by Vaughan's reading of mystical and hermetic literature.

l. 2 *like a great ring:* Felltham, in *Resolves*, writing 'Of Time's continual speed', describes Virtues and Vices engaged in conflict to gain the human soul, 'and behind all these came Eternity, casting a Ring about them, which like a strong enchantment, made them for ever the same'.

l. 16 *the darksome statesman:* possibly alluding to Oliver Cromwell.

ll. 23–25 Cf. Herbert, *Confession:*
>   Like moles within us, heave and cast about
>   And till they foot and clutch their prey
>   They never cool, much less give out.

l. 38 *placed heav'n in sense:* found heaven in the satisfaction of his senses.

ll. 44–45 Cf. Herbert, *The Church Militant:*
>   While Truth sat by, counting his victories.

ll. 51–54 *grots and caves:* reminiscent of the allegory of the Cave in Plato's *Republic*, VII.

p. 148 *Man*

Grierson finds in this poem 'the essence of the thought which Wordsworth returned to with such imaginative passion after the storm and stress of revolutionary hopes and disappointments', the divine harmony and joy of nature contrasted with the unhappiness and instability of man. The last two stanzas are closely paralleled in Herbert's *Giddiness*.

l. 23 *stones:* lodestones, symbolizing the 'wit' and life in objects seemingly inanimate.

p. 149 *Cock-crowing*

Miss Mahood calls attention to the technical, esoteric words 'glance', 'ray', and 'tincture' near the opening of the poem, clarifying their meaning by quoting from Thomas Vaughan's *Anima Magica Abscondita:* 'The soul . . . is guided in her operations by a spiritual, metaphysical grain, a seed or glance of light, and simple and without any mixture, descending from the First Father of Lights.'

l. 1 *Father of lights.* 'Every good gift and every perfect gift is from above, and cometh down from the Father of lights.' *James*, I. 17.

l. 10 *house of light:* cf. the title of Thomas Vaughan's *Aula Lucis, Or, the House of Light.* 1652.

ll. 11, 12 cf. 'This is the secret candle of God, which he hath tinn'd in the Elements', Thomas Vaughan, *Lumen de Lumine*, 1651.

ll. 20–22 Based upon *Rom.*, I. 20, 21.

l. 29 *dark, Egyptian border:* refers to the plague of darkness. *Exod.*, X. 21–23.

ll. 37–41 *this veil.* The veil, a favourite image of Vaughan's, here represents human flesh. The rending of the veil symbolizes resurrection. Cf. *Matt.*, XXVII. 51, II *Cor.*, III. 13, 14.

l. 41 *Thy full-eyed love.* Cf. Herbert, *The Glance:*

> What wonders shall we feel when we shall see
> > Thy full-eyed love!

and Thomas Vaughan, *Anima Magica Recondita*, 1650, 'his full-ey'd love shines on nothing but Man'.

l. 48 *no lily.* Cf. 'My beloved is mine and I am his; he feedeth among the lilies.' *Song of Solomon*, II. 16.

p. 151 *The Bird*

The directness and simplicity of the message carried in the bird's 'early hymns' are reflected in simple and homely language. The concept of the song as a devotional act is emphasized through its association with such words and phrases as 'hymns', 'praise and prayer', 'solemn matins'.

l. 19 The same notion recurs in 'They are all gone into the world of light', ll. 29–32.

p. 152 *The Timber*

The poet's point of departure is the familiar hermetic theory of secret energy residing within objects of nature seemingly inanimate, but the basic image of timber tends to be lost as the poem proceeds.

l. 19 *resentment:* used in the literal sense of 'feeling back', i.e. responsive feeling.

l. 50 *Begetting virgins.* Alternative interpretations suggested are primroses and *agnus castus.* The emendation of 'virgins' to 'verdure' is unnecessary and inconsistent with the sense of the two following lines.

p. 154 *The Rainbow*

ll. 3–8, and 18 The allusion is to *Gen.,* IX. 13–17, and the names are taken from *Gen.,* IX, X, and XI.

l. 11 *Rain gently spends his honey-drops.* Cf. Herbert, *Providence:*
Rain, do not hurt my flowers; but gently spend
Your honey drops.

p. 155 *Childhood*

Comparable throughout with *The Retreat,* and likewise anticipating Wordsworth's notions of childhood.

l. 4 *white designs:* Cf. *The Retreat,* 6, and note p. 231.

l. 16 *medicinal.* Cf. Herbert, who frequently alludes to the medicinal properties of flowers, with religious overtones, e.g. in *Life:*
Farewell, dear flowers, sweetly your time ye spent,
Fit while ye lived for smell or ornament,
And after death for cures.

p. 157 *The Waterfall*

An outstanding specimen of Vaughan's artistry in applying a religious motive to detailed description of natural objects. He may be referring specifically to the Rhydgoch, or Red Fall, near his home. 'The water seems to pause on the brink of the fall, and seems afraid, just as the soul is afraid, when it approaches death. Nevertheless, the soul, like the water, will rise.' (Leishman.)

l. 38 *My glorious liberty.* 'Because the creature itself also shall be delivered from the bondage of corruption into the glorious liberty of the children of God.' *Rom.,* VIII. 21.

p. 158 *'They are all gone into the world of light'*

Referring, perhaps, specifically to Vaughan's younger brother,

William, who died in 1648, and to his first wife, as well as to the friends, to whose memory he dedicated *Olor Iscanus*.

l. 9 *walking in an air of glory*. The comparison is with 'demons of the air', spirits believed to inhabit the upper air, of an intermediate rank between angels and devils, and undisturbed by atmosphere or celestial motions. They are referred to frequently by hermetic and Neo-Platonic writers, and incidentally by others: as 'eyryssh bestes', by Chaucer (*House of Fame*, II. 932) and by Dryden (*The Hind and the Panther*, I. 341–2) as

spirits of a middle sort,
Too black for heav'n, and yet too white for hell.

l. 38 *pérspective:* telescope, stressed on the first syllable.
l. 40 *glass:* telescope.

ANDREW MARVELL (1621–1678)

The son of an Anglican clergyman, Marvell was born at Winestead, Yorks., and educated at the Grammar School, Hull, where his father was Master of the Charterhouse, and at Trinity College, Cambridge, where he resided from 1633 to 1640. During the next four years he travelled abroad, and in 1651 became tutor to Lord Fairfax's daughter, residing with the Fairfax family for two years at Nunappleton House, Yorkshire, where probably most of his best-known secular work was written. In 1653 he became tutor to Cromwell's ward, William Dutton, living at Eton in the house of John Oxenbridge, a Fellow of the College, who had previously acted as minister in the Bermudas. In 1657 he was appointed to assist Milton as Latin Secretary, the latter having already recommended him for the post four years earlier as a man 'of singular desert for the State to make use of'. The following year he was elected one of two members of Parliament for Hull, holding his seat until his death twenty years later. During this period he printed anonymously a succession of political satires attacking the government policy and leaders in court and parliament. The first collection of his poems was published fraudulently in 1681 through the machinations of Mary Palmer, Marvell's housekeeper at the time of his death, who claimed to be his widow.

All the poems by which Marvell is generally remembered reflect the tranquillity and gracious living of an English country house, where, in fact, most of them were written. Though supporting the Parliamentary party and serving under its leaders, he may, in the first instance, have been driven to this course through circumstance or reasons of expediency rather than through natural inclination, for his early work is devoid of any political bias; the most memorable passage in the *Horatian Ode* to Cromwell is his moving tribute to King Charles's behaviour on the scaffold. In his other early poems Marvell imparts new life to old conventions, more particularly to the pastoral, which he adapts, under different guises and for different ends, in the 'Mower' poems, *The Garden*, and *The Nymph Complaining for the Death of her Faun*. Arcadia gives place to the English scene and the English country estate. There are many parallels between Marvell's poetry and that of his contemporaries, particularly Crashaw and Cowley, but its metaphysical quality shows in his taste for syllogism and rhetorical devices rather than in violent turns of imagery. His poetry reflects the transition from the Jacobean and Caroline 'fantastic' to the ingenious gentleman of the Augustan age.

p. 160 *The Nymph Complaining for the Death of her Faun*
Elegies on the deaths of pet birds by Catullus, Ovid, and Skelton provide well-known antetypes to this poem. A nearer approach, both chronologically and in subject, is the description of Fida's dismay at the slaying of her hind in Browne's *Britannia's Pastorals*, I. 4. Marvell characteristically imparts to the familiar theme new overtones of meaning, the child's grief at her loss being associated with sensuous affection, desertion by a false lover, and martyred innocence.

l. 1 *troopers:* engaged in the Civil War.
l. 17 *Deodands.* Moveable properties occasioning death were forfeited to the lord of the manor, to be given to charity, and therefore to God.
ll. 31–6 Antithesis between the faithful and the faithless is a leading motive in the poem. The dramatic irony of the puns on 'deer' and 'heart' is heightened if the nymph is unaware of them.

ll. 71–92 Cf. *Song of Sol.*, II. 16, 17, IV. 5, 6, VI. 2, 3.

l. 99 *Heliades:* daughters of Helios, the Sun-God, sisters of Phaeton.

ll. 111–118 Cf. the figure employed by Browne in his *Epitaph on the Countess of Pembroke*, 9–12, p. 32.

p. 163 *Bermudas*

In 1653 Marvell acted as tutor to Cromwell's ward, William Dutton, at Eton, and lived in the house of John Oxenbridge, Fellow of the College, who had twice visited the Bermudas, discovered by Juan Bermudez in 1515.

l. 9 *sea-monsters:* whales.

ll. 13–24 This idealized description is paralleled in Captain John Smith's *The General History of Virginia, New England, and the Summer Isles*, 1624, where special note is made of the permanence of spring in the Summer Isles (Bermudas).

l. 20 *Ormus:* Hormuz, on the Persian Gulf.

l. 21 Cf. *The Garden*, 36.

l. 23 *apples:* pineapples.

l. 28 *ambergris:* a waxy substance, found in whales, and floating in tropical seas, odoriferous, and used in perfumery (from French *ombre gris*).

p. 164 *To his Coy Mistress*

The poem is based on the favourite 'Carpe diem' motive, developed with Marvell's characteristic ingenuity and wit. The dramatic character of argument and counter-argument is sharpened with the aid of rhetorical figures, and enlivened through steadily accelerating metrical pace.

l. 7 *Humber*. The stroke of local colour induces a down-to-earth realism violently contrasted with the far-fetched fantasy of 'Indian Ganges' and the hyperbolical imagery of the ensuing lines.

l. 24 'With modern spelling and pronunciation the threefold 'ah' sound in this line is lost:

Desarts of vast Etarnity'. (Margoliouth.)

l. 34 *dew*. The original printed version reads 'glew', possibly for 'glow', but no parallel to this word as a noun is known. Margoliouth suggests as a possibility 'lew', meaning warmth, and cites seventeenth-century parallels; but 'dew' is the reading generally accepted.

l. 40 *his slow-chapt pow'r:* the power of his slowly-devouring jaws.

ll. 45, 46 The paradox effectively clinches the antithetical argument that has led up to it.

p. 166 *Damon the Mower*

l. 12 *hamstring'd:* crippled, strictly by cutting the tendon at the back of the knee or hind leg.

l. 48 *cowslip water.* The juice of cowslips was used to cleanse the skin from spots and to remove wrinkles.

l. 83 *shepherd's-purse, and clown's-all-heal:* the former a common weed (Capsella Bursa pastoris), the latter the marsh woundwort, both regarded as remedies against bleeding.

p. 169 *The Mower to the Glow-worms*

l. 9 *officious:* zealous, attentive.

p. 169 *The Gallery*

l. 11 *examining:* testing.

l. 48 Charles I bought the entire collection of Vincenzo Gonzaga, Duke of Mantua, and added it to his collection at Whitehall.

p. 171 *The Garden*

Marvell wrote a Latin poem on the same theme, entitled *Hortus*, probably at about the same time as *The Garden*. Though there are close correspondences between the two versions, neither is a close translation of the other.

ll. 1–16 The two opening stanzas establish one of the main motives of the poem, the contrast between the active and the contemplative life.

l. 2 *palm:* symbolizes victory in general, a crown of *oak*-leaves was awarded to a soldier who had saved the life of a Roman citizen, and a wreath of *bay*-leaves or laurel to a poet.

ll. 17–24 *White* and *red*, conventional symbols of feminine beauty, are contrasted with *green*, the colour of nature, which far exceeds such beauty. From this point onwards Marvell proceeds to focus attention more and more on symbolical green and its significance.

l. 28 *did end their race.* The pun enforces the double meaning.

ll. 27–32 Daphne, the daughter of the river-god, Peneus, was pursued by Apollo, but, appealing to Zeus, was changed into a laurel tree. Syrinx, an Arcadian nymph, pursued by Pan, was changed into a reed, from which he made his pipes.

l. 37 *curious:* used in its literal sense, 'requiring care', hence 'exquisite', 'choice'.

ll. 43, 44 One of the 'Vulgar Errors' discussed by Sir Thomas Browne in *Pseudodoxia Epidemica* was 'that all Animals of the Land are in their kind in the Sea'.

ll. 47, 48 The general sense of this famous and much discussed line is clear enough: 'annihilating', or 'sublimating' the material world, creating instead a world transcending material objects, figured as 'a green thought'.

l. 54 *whets:* preens.

l. 66 A flower dial was a flower-bed planted with flowers opening and closing at different times, thus serving to tell the time. Linnæus constructed such a dial, consisting of forty-six different species of flowers.

p. 173 *An Horatian Ode*

Cromwell returned from Ireland in May 1650, and entered Scotland two months later. Marvell's poem, written after Cromwell's return and referring to the impending campaign in Scotland, must therefore have been composed during the intervening weeks. It expresses, apparently, the attitude of a 'liberal parliamentarian', who, while recognizing the courage of King Charles, saw in Cromwell the present hope of the nation. The ode is 'Horatian' in virtue of its diction, style, and verse-form, an imitation from the four-line stanza frequently used by Horace.

ll. 23, 24 Laurels were believed to be proof against lightning. The lines may also allude to the representation of the King's head, surrounded by a laurel wreath, on recently issued gold coins.

ll. 29, 30 Cromwell lived a quiet life in the neighbourhood of St. Ives, Hunts., until the election of the Long Parliament, when he was forty-one.

l. 32 *bergamot:* a fine species of pear.

l. 42 *penetration.* A term of natural philosophy, applied to 'a supposed or conceived occupation of the same space by two bodies at the same time'. (O.E.D.)

ll. 47–52 Charles I fled from Hampton Court to Carisbrooke on 11 November 1647, and it was alleged that Cromwell had connived at the King's escape in his own interests.

l. 52 *case:* plight, or cage.

ll. 67–72 When the temple of Jupiter was founded on the Tarpeian hill in Rome, a human head, with face intact, was unearthed. This was regarded as a favourable omen for Rome.

ll. 77–80 A fiction of flattery, for which there is no evidence.

l. 104 *climacteric:* making a climax, critical.

l. 106 *particolour'd:* a pun on the derivation of Pict, from *pinctus.*

l. 117 *the force it has to fright:* alluding to the cross-hilt of the sword, empowered to avert the spirits of night.

FURTHER READING

Texts

The Clarendon Press editions listed provide authoritative texts, with full introductions and notes.

BROWNE, WILLIAM, *Poems*, 2 vols., ed. by Gordon Goodwin, with an Introduction by A. H. Bullen (1894), (The Muses' Library) Routledge. Includes some brief notes.

CAREW, THOMAS, *Poems*, ed. by Rhodes Dunlap (1949), Clarendon Press.

CRASHAW, RICHARD, *Poems*, ed. by L. C. Martin (1957), Clarendon Press.

HERBERT, GEORGE, *Works*, ed. by F. E. Hutchinson (1953), Clarendon Press.

HERRICK, ROBERT, *Poetical Works*, ed. by L. C. Martin (1956), Clarendon Press.

JONSON, BEN, *Ben Jonson*, 11 vols., ed. by C. H. Herford and Percy Simpson (1925–52), Clarendon Press. Parts of vols. II, VIII, and XI relate to Jonson's non-dramatic poetry.

LOVELACE, RICHARD, *Poems*, ed. by C. H. Wilkinson (1953), Clarendon Press.

MARVELL, ANDREW, *Poems and Letters*, 2 vols., ed. by H. M. Margoliouth (1952), Clarendon Press. Vol. I contains Marvell's Poems.

MILTON, JOHN, *Poetical Works*, 3 vols. ed. by David Masson (1890), Macmillan. *Poetical Works*, ed. by Douglas Bush (1966), Oxford University Press. Masson's edition, providing extensive commentaries and notes, remains authoritative. Bush's one-volume edition includes useful compact notes.

SUCKLING, SIR JOHN, *Works*, ed. by A. Hamilton Thompson (1910), Routledge. Includes some brief notes.

VAUGHAN, HENRY, *Works* (1957), ed. by L. C. Martin, Clarendon Press.

Criticism

Bennett, Joan, *Five Metaphysical Poets* (1964), Cambridge University Press.

Bush, Douglas, *English Literature in the Earlier Seventeenth*

Century, Second edition (1962), Clarendon Press. A volume of the Oxford History of English Literature, invaluable for background study, and including a full bibliography.

Daiches, David, *Milton* (1957), Hutchinson University Library.

Grierson, Herbert J. C., *Metaphysical Lyrics and Poems of the Seventeenth Century*, selected and edited, with an Essay (1921, etc.), Clarendon Press. The introductory essay and notes are suggestive, and by no means outmoded.

Johnston, G. B., *Ben Jonson: Poet* (1945), Columbia University Press.

Keast, William, *Seventeenth-Century English Poetry* (1962), a Galaxy Book, Oxford University Press. Includes reprints of essays on Jonson, Herbert, Crashaw, Lovelace, and Marvell.

Leishman, J. B., *Metaphysical Poets* (1934), Clarendon Press. Includes studies of Herbert and Vaughan. *The Art of Marvell's Poetry* (1966), Hutchinson.

Mahood, M. M., *Poetry and Humanism* (1950), Cape. Throws light on Renaissance influences reflected in seventeenth-century metaphysical poetry.

Willey, Basil, *The Seventeenth-Century Background* (1934), Chatto and Windus.

INDEX OF FIRST LINES